United Methodism at Forty

United Methodism at Forty

Looking Back
Looking Forward

CHARLES YRIGOYEN JR.
JOHN G. McELLHENNEY
KENNETH E. ROWE

Abingdon Press
Nashville

UNITED METHODISM AT FORTY
LOOKING BACK, LOOKING FORWARD

Library of Congress Cataloging-in-Publication Data

Yrigoyen, Charles, 1937-
    United Methodism at forty : looking back, looking forward / Charles Yrigoyen, Jr., John G. McEllhenney, Kenneth E. Rowe.
        p. cm.
    Includes bibliographical references.
    ISBN 978-0-687-65129-0 (pbk. : alk. paper)
    1. United Methodist Church (U.S.)—History.   I. McEllhenney, John Galen.   II. Rowe, Kenneth E.   III. Title.
    BX8237.Y75 2008
    287′.6—dc22

                                                                                            2007047716

08 09 10 11 12 13 14 15 16 17—10 9 8 7 6 5 4 3 2 1

MANUFACTURED IN THE UNITED STATES OF AMERICA

In memory of

Frederick E. Maser, D.D. (1908–2002)

Clergyman, historian, philanthropist, bibliophile,

and quintessential Methodist—

friend on earth and friend above

Contents

PREFACE

All three of us were pastors in the Methodist Church before its union with the Evangelical United Brethren in 1968 and have lived through the first forty years of United Methodism. We are clergy members of the same annual conference, Eastern Pennsylvania, and longtime friends. Each of us has taught United Methodist history, doctrine, and polity—courses required of those seeking ordination—in various theological seminaries, including those that are not affiliated with The United Methodist Church. Together we coauthored a brief history of the denomination, *Proclaiming Grace and Freedom: The Story of United Methodism in America* (Nashville: Abingdon Press, 1982), for Methodism's 1984 bicentennial. A revised edition of that book, *United Methodism in America: A Compact History* (Nashville: Abingdon Press, 1992), was published a decade later and remains in print. A fourth coauthor, Frederick E. Maser, accomplished Methodist historian and cherished friend who died in 2002, assisted with both the original and revised editions of that book. We publish this book in his memory.

We owe a major debt of gratitude to Rex D. Matthews, faculty member of Candler School of Theology, Emory University, in whose mind the idea for this book was conceived, and to Robert A. Ratcliff and the staff of the United Methodist Publishing House who have brought it into print.

There are numerous colleagues, librarians, archivists, church agencies, and friends who have contributed to our work. Among them are Chris Anderson, Chris Beldan, Richard Berg, Scott R. Brewer, Robert F. Kohler, Terry M. Heisey, Julie A. Miller, Iain D. Murton, L. Dale Patterson, Darryl W. Stephens, and the deaconess staff of the General Board of Global Ministries. Countless others have shaped our ideas and provided information. To all of them we offer our gratitude.

Charles Yrigoyen Jr.
John G. McEllhenney
Kenneth E. Rowe

CHAPTER 1

HISTORICAL ROOTS OF UNITED METHODISM'S UNION

The United Methodist Church was created in 1968 by a union of the Methodist Church and the Evangelical United Brethren Church. Both uniting denominations were mergers of former churches. In 1939 a Methodist union brought together the Methodist Episcopal Church; the Methodist Protestant Church; and the Methodist Episcopal Church, South. The Evangelical United Brethren Church was formed in 1946 when the Evangelical Church and the Church of the United Brethren in Christ constituted a new denomination. What follows is a brief historical overview of the origins and development of the two churches that formed United Methodism, including points of contact between their predecessors over the years. It places the denominational union into a wider historical context.

Methodism is deeply rooted in the eighteenth-century evangelical revival in England and in the ministry of John Wesley (1703–91) and his younger brother Charles (1707–88). Born and raised in Epworth, England, by their father, Samuel, a Church of England clergyman, and their devout mother, Susanna, the brothers were classically educated at Oxford University, ordained into the priesthood of the Church of England, together were short-term missionaries to the American colony of Georgia, and had transforming religious experiences in May 1738. In the years following, thousands were influenced by their gospel preaching. Those who desired to follow the Wesleyan pattern of discipleship were organized into Methodist societies each of which was composed of smaller groups for worship, fellowship, nurture, and ministry.

At its beginning the Wesleyan brand of Methodism was intended not to be a church, but a renewal movement within the Church of England under the leadership of the Wesley brothers. John was the movement's principal theological leader, writer, preacher, and organizer. Charles, also an effective preacher, was its poet, much of his work surviving today in the hymn books of almost every Christian church.

Major emphasis in the Wesleys' understanding of the Christian faith was placed on the transforming grace of God and free human response to it in holiness of heart and life—loving God with all one is and has, and loving neighbor, which included everyone, as oneself. The holiness that the Wesleys proclaimed in word and song was nurtured by Bible study, prayer, the Lord's Supper, worship, and Christian fellowship. Holy living, the result of a life transformed and sustained by God's grace, was both personal and social. It was demonstrated in works of ministry such as feeding the hungry, clothing the naked, welcoming the homeless, and visiting the sick and imprisoned (Matthew 25:31-46). John Wesley established a pattern of social engagement by establishing free medical clinics at his chapels, giving generously to the poor, visiting prisons, opposing slavery, founding a school, and providing shelter for widows and orphaned children.

Methodism was organized in America in the 1760s by laypeople, immigrants from Ireland and England. As the movement took hold in the colonies, John Wesley dispatched lay missionary-preachers to supervise its growth. One of these missionary-preachers was Francis Asbury (1745–1816), who with Thomas Coke (1747–1814) became American Methodism's primary leaders. In 1784 Wesley assented to the request of the American Methodists to form a church, which they organized in Baltimore, Maryland, at what is known as the Christmas Conference. The new body was named the Methodist Episcopal Church and grew significantly during its earlier decades. Matters of governance and race, however, caused divisions, two of which were the Methodist Protestant Church and the Methodist Episcopal Church, South. These three—the Methodist Episcopal Church; the Methodist Protestant Church; and the Methodist Episcopal Church, South—were rejoined in 1939 as the Methodist Church.[1]

Predecessors of the Evangelical United Brethren Church were the Church of the United Brethren in Christ and the Evangelical Church.

Both were born in the evangelical experiences of their founders and a desire to minister to the spiritual needs of the German-speaking inhabitants after the United States became a nation.[2]

Philip William Otterbein (1726–1813) and Martin Boehm (1725–1812) founded the United Brethren tradition. Otterbein, university educated at Herborn, a Pietist school in Germany that emphasized a personal experience of God's grace, was ordained in the German Reformed Church; commissioned as a missionary to America, arriving in 1752; and began a pastorate in Lancaster, Pennsylvania. While serving there his ministry was permanently changed by a fresh experience of God's redemptive love. Later, in a revival meeting at Isaac Long's barn near Lancaster in 1767, Otterbein heard the preaching of Martin Boehm, a Mennonite. Profoundly moved by Boehm's sermon, he approached the Anabaptist preacher, embraced him, and declared, *"Wir sind brüder!"* ("We are brethren!"). This encounter marks the beginning of their important partnership and is considered a key event in United Brethren history. Otterbein's ministry culminated in a forty-year pastorate to a German Reformed congregation in Baltimore, Maryland, which began in 1774. There his program for church renewal blossomed and he became the leader of an evangelical movement among German preachers.

Martin Boehm was born of Mennonite parents in Lancaster County, Pennsylvania. For a time he was a Mennonite bishop. Sometime before his meeting with Otterbein in 1767, Boehm experienced a personal assurance of God's presence and power, which led him to preach with new confidence and enthusiasm.

After their 1767 meeting at Long's barn both Otterbein and Boehm proclaimed a message of God's love in Christ and gradually gathered people into groups whose desire was to worship and serve with others of a similar mind. A few were convinced of God's call to preach and desired to unite under the direction of Otterbein and Boehm. In 1800, thirteen preachers, including Otterbein and Boehm, met in a private home in Frederick, Maryland; constituted themselves a church; and agreed to meet annually. Otterbein and Boehm were chosen to superintend the ministry of the new church. A *Book of Discipline* was adopted in 1815, and following the deaths of the two leaders the influence of the church matured and expanded under the direction of Christian Newcomer (1749–1830).

The Church of the United Brethren in Christ was divided in 1889 over a modification of its constitution and the church's position on secret societies, especially membership in the Freemasons. Those who wished to retain the present constitution and prohibit membership to those who were members of secret societies separated to form the Church of the United Brethren in Christ (Old Constitution). Bishop Milton Wright, father of Orville and Wilbur, was a leader of the seceding group.

Jacob Albright (1759–1808), who had been raised Lutheran in eastern Pennsylvania, was the founder of the Evangelical Church. A farmer, tile-maker, and Revolutionary War veteran, Albright had a conversion experience in 1791 and afterward was nurtured by Methodists in one of their small group meetings. Albright's deep concern for the spiritual condition of the churchless German-speaking led him into a preaching ministry. He formed three small groups in 1800 and seven years later gathered some of his leading followers, including those called to preach, in Kleinfeltersville, Pennsylvania, to organize a church. Albright was chosen its first bishop. In 1816 the church formally adopted the name *Evangelische Gemeinschaft* (Evangelical Association). One of their most important leaders was John Seybert (1791–1860), the second bishop of the church and renowned for his ministry of outreach resulting in the church's extending growth and influence.

A number of issues, including the nature of holiness, the use of English for worship and church publications, and personality conflicts among the church's leaders, led to a division in the church in 1892 when a seceding group organized the United Evangelical Church. The two bodies reunited in 1922 to become the Evangelical Church, but a significant number of the former United Evangelical Church did not join this union and formed the Evangelical Congregational Church.[3]

United Brethren and Evangelicals considered union as far back as the early nineteenth century when United Brethren bishop Christian Newcomer proposed merger on repeated visits to Evangelical meetings. After all, the two were similar in both organization and doctrine. Overtures in 1924 by the United Brethren were met with favor, although the Evangelicals were in the midst of reordering their life following their own 1922 union. Evangelical bishop M. T. Maze, fraternal delegate to the 1933 United Brethren General Conference, invited a new consideration of organic union between the two churches. After several years of thorough negotiation, which took place amid the clamor of world war, the merger was finally accomplished in 1946.

Methodists and Evangelical United Brethren had a history of interrelationship long before their 1968 marriage, especially in the earlier years of their histories. On the United Brethren side, Francis Asbury's journal records several references to Otterbein beginning in 1774. Over the ensuing years Asbury visited and traveled with him, preached in his Baltimore church, and occasionally conversed with him about ministry among the German-speaking.[4] Otterbein assisted at Asbury's ordination by laying on hands at the Christmas Conference on Monday, December 27, 1784. Twenty-nine years later Methodists reciprocated when William Ryland, one of their elders, assisted Otterbein with the first three ordinations in the United Brethren Church.[5] Following Otterbein's death in 1813, Asbury eulogized his friend at a session of the Baltimore annual conference in which he said, "Forty years have I known the retiring modesty of this man of God; towering above his fellows in learning, wisdom, and grace, yet seeking to be known only of God and the people of God."[6] Although Asbury apparently did not have the same intimate friendship with Martin Boehm, one of Asbury's most trusted friends and traveling companions was Henry Boehm, one of Martin's sons.[7] At Martin Boehm's funeral Asbury expressed disappointment that both Otterbein and Boehm did not exercise sufficient authority over their church. In Asbury's opinion they would have formed a stronger church had they followed the provisions of the Methodist *Discipline*.[8] Unwillingness to surrender their commitment to German language for worship and governance, the nature of episcopal authority, and the absence of a formal book of discipline were among issues that kept United Brethren and Methodism separate.[9]

On the Evangelical side, we have already noted that following his conversion Jacob Albright was nurtured in a Methodist class meeting. He was granted a Methodist exhorter's license in 1796, which enabled him to speak in class meetings. "Gradually," however, "he allowed his Methodist affiliations, including his exhorter's license, to lapse."[10] Methodist influence among the Evangelicals continued when they used the Methodist *Discipline* and Articles of Religion as a pattern for their own book of order and Articles of Faith.[11]

Affiliation among United Brethren, Evangelicals, and Methodists in local communities encouraged relationships, and their common membership in the Federal Council of Churches (later the National Council of Churches) and the World Council of Churches was another important factor in preparing the way for their 1968 union.

—꿈— —꿈— —꿈— —꿈— —꿈— —꿈— —꿈— —꿈—

For further reading, see John G. McEllhenney, ed., *United Methodism in America: A Compact History* (Nashville: Abingdon Press, 1992), a readable narrative of the origins and development of United Methodism and its predecessors in the United States; Russell E. Richey, Kenneth E. Rowe, and Jean Miller Schmidt, *The Methodist Experience in America: A Sourcebook* (Nashville: Abingdon Press, 2000), a valuable collection of primary sources containing important documents related to the formation of United Methodism (especially pages 611-706); and Charles Yrigoyen Jr. and Susan E. Warrick, eds., *Historical Dictionary of Methodism* (Lanham, Md.: Scarecrow Press, 2005), which contains short articles on important personalities, doctrines, and events in Methodism, the Evangelical Church, and the United Brethren.

CHAPTER 2

OVERVIEW AND CONTEXT

U nited Methodism moved along its first forty years as if treading
through cultural and historical molasses. Each step meant trying
to pull its feet out of this sticky context—to be true to God, not
the passing age. Always, however, aspects of the times stuck to its positions and actions. This chapter offers an overview of United Methodist
history within its cultural and historical context.

The Methodist and Evangelical United Brethren churches united at
the very time, 1968, when America seemed to be splitting. In 1963, Lee
Harvey Oswald gunned down President John F. Kennedy in Dallas, Texas,
five years before a conference convened there to usher in The United
Methodist Church. Just days prior to the conference's opening, Dr.
Martin Luther King Jr. was murdered in Memphis, Tennessee.
Unification was scarcely a month old when an assassin killed presidential
aspirant Robert F. Kennedy in Los Angeles, California. And riots fired by
racial tensions charred sections of American cities in 1967 and 1968,
while student antiwar protests during the same period widened the divide
between pro- and anti-Vietnam War Americans, forecasting the ran-
corous divide over President George W. Bush's Iraq War that characterized the United States as United Methodism approached its fortieth
birthday.

During early May 1968, as delegates to the uniting conference debated
the plan of union for United Methodism crafted by lawyer and financier
Charles C. Parlin,[1] university students in Paris were rebelling against the
order and restraint fostered by lawyers and financiers. One of their graf-
fiti slogans was Sous les pavés, la plage: "Beneath the paving stones, the
beach."[2] Using the ancient cobblestones of Paris as a symbol, they were

saying that by ripping up the age-old certainties of politicians, industrial-ists, lawyers, educators, financiers, and priests, it would be possible to live their lives as if they were dancing almost naked on the beach to the ele-mental beat of the surf. Within weeks, however, Parisian forces of order and restraint were slathering tarmac on the Latin Quarter's cobblestones, depriving the students of their antiestablishment projectiles and fore-shadowing a tactic used by traditionalists in decades to come—the impo-sition of black-and-white solutions on multicolored situations.[3]

Meanwhile in Dallas, at the uniting conference, a Methodist professor spotlighted the cultural and political upheavals that Europeans now call *sixty-eight-ism*. Professor Albert Outler, an authority on the theology of John Wesley, told the uniters that "the world is in furious and agonizing turmoil, incomprehensible and unmanageable. The church is in radical crisis, and in the throes of a profound demoralization, at every level: of faith and order, life and work. In such times, business as usual simply will not get our business done."[4] Business as usual, however, did get the busi-ness of uniting done. Yes and no votes were counted on proposals reading like legal documents, and the conference approved a plan of union that provided a hierarchical structure for the new denomination—a structure that tightly connected its local, regional, national, and world levels.

One dimension of Outler's "radical crisis"—racism—was foremost in the minds of the uniters. The previous summer, because of race riots, had been hotter than usual. In 1968, the Kerner Commission, appointed by President Lyndon Johnson to investigate civil disorders, declared the United States was "moving toward two societies, one black, one white—separate and unequal."[5] The same year, Congress passed a civil rights act that outlawed discrimination in the sale, rental, or financing of housing. Voting in that atmosphere, members of the uniting conference approved a plan of union that eliminated the Central Jurisdiction of the former Methodist Church, in which black churches and annual conferences were separated from white Methodist congregations and conferences in the same areas; however, it took another five years for annual conferences to integrate. To keep United Methodists attentive to achieving racial equality, the General Commission on Religion and Race was added to the list of national agencies.

Outler, in his sermon on the day when The United Methodist Church was born, said: "Obviously, no part of our venture in unity is really *finished* as yet!" Ample evidence lay before the uniters. When dealing with United Methodist doctrine, the plan of union placed the Methodist

Articles of Religion and Evangelical United Brethren Confession of Faith side by side, declaring that they were "congruent if not identical in their doctrinal perspectives."[6] Similar was the handling of the statements of social principles of the two uniting denominations, and the hymnals and rituals of both previous churches were approved for use in the new one. Although the national boards of the two churches were consolidated, a more efficient structure was conceivable. So a structure study was authorized, as were studies of the new church's doctrine and social principles, and projects for reshaping the church's rituals were put in motion.

These studies were undertaken in unsettled and unsettling times. Top structures of any kind and their bureaucracies were distrusted by men and women who came of age in the sixties. Theological windows had been opened and, in some cases, smashed during the same decade. Agendas for liberating theology from white male captivity drew alleluias from many, but not all, throats. Serious attention was given to the theological perspectives of women, persons of color, and non-Western Christians. Although many unlocked and opened theological windows during the 1960s, others, especially toward the end of the decade, tried to slam them shut and click their locks. In 1966, Methodist pastor Charles Keysor spoke for "the silent minority" in Methodism "who are orthodox." A year later, his manifesto led to the organization of the window-closing "Good News" movement.

The social principles study group began working during the era of the Hippies, who "stressed cooperation instead of competition, sexual freedom instead of puritanical restrictions, sharing instead of hoarding resources, and freedom to be one's own self and do one's own thing rather than bondage to tradition."[7] In due course, this counterculture program entered the mainstream. *The Graduate* (1967), a screening of seduction and adultery, was one of the top ten films of the sixties, and the 1969 Oscar for best picture went to the X-rated, gay-themed film *Midnight Cowboy*. That same year, the Stonewall Riots in the Greenwich Village section of New York City brought the cause of gay rights to national attention. In October 1968, a student protest against the Vietnam War at the University of Wisconsin prompted protests across the nation. Many congregations were divided between those who denounced the protesters as traitors to their country and those who supported them as truth-tellers about the war. Against this background of political and social upheaval, United Methodism revised its social principles.

The uniting conference of 1968, having established study commissions to reshape the church's structure and to recommend ways to handle social principles and doctrine, launched The United Methodist Church. For its navigational plan, it had a Constitution, a *Book of Discipline*, and official resolutions on various subjects. Armed with these navigational aids, persons at the church's helm attempted to sail on cultural currents flowing out of the 1960s—the currents of liberation, inclusion, autonomy, participation, and globalization. Then, after 1975, they had to pay close attention to an anti-sixties countercurrent.

Five Cultural Currents of the Sixties

During the first forty years of their history, United Methodists dealt with five cultural currents, each of which had begun to flow strongly by the mid sixties. Liberation is listed here as one of the five. Yet there is a potent element of freedom in each of the other four—freedom *from* old oppressions, freedom *for* new possibilities: "Beneath the paving stones, the beach."

The *current of liberation*, examined separately, promoted freedom from white male domination of culture, education, government, business, and religion. Freedom *from*: poverty, "Jim Crow" laws, restraints on sexual expression, restricted opportunities for women, unthinking obedience to government, and handed-down theology. Freedom *to be*: black *and* beautiful, gay *and* proud, a professional woman *and* a mother, a patriot *and* a draft-resister, a doubter *and* a believer.

During the succeeding decades, there were, broadly speaking, two United Methodist responses to the current of liberation: center-right United Methodists held that liberation was a current flowing in the wrong direction, that it must be redirected, if not dammed; center-left United Methodists maintained that the current of liberation was flowing into a better future, especially for persons of color, women, and homosexuals.

Second, from its birth, The United Methodist Church sailed on the *current of inclusion*—liberation from a variety of exclusions. The year the church was born, 1968, a federal agency ruled that help-wanted ads that, in effect, excluded females from certain jobs were illegal. Vigorous efforts were made by the church to include women and racial and ethnic minorities at every level of its life. An equally vigorous campaign to replace male-gender words with inclusive language in all references to human beings was, after heated debates, successful. A similar attempt to substitute inclusive for male-gender words when speaking about God met fierce resistance, but by the early twenty-first century, it had racked up a few minor victories.

United Methodism, third, tacked against the *current of autonomy*, which emphasized the self-determining individual. The young of the 1960s admonished everyone "to do their own thing." United Methodists, however, programmed as they are by Wesleyan DNA, resisted my-way-ism. Followers of John Wesley make decisions *in conference* about what to teach and what to do. Then they put their decisions to work at the grassroots. The Constitution of The United Methodist Church, adopted in 1968, asserts that the annual conference, not the local church, is the "fundamental," the "basic"[8] body of the church. Across the next forty years, United Methodist leaders worked to preserve this connectionalism, while also providing some freedom, under strict guidelines, for annual conferences and local churches to organize for mission in their own ways.

Fourth, persons who voted for the first time during the late sixties rowed with the *current of participation*. They participated in civil rights marches, burned draft cards during antiwar protests, and danced at mass music events. The 1969 Woodstock Festival supplied one of the names for this generation, which included women and men who walked out of church when expected to be passive pew-sitters.

The current of participation transformed the way the true is defined and the newsworthy is determined. Until the closing years of the twentieth century, the true and the newsworthy were the preserve of a few authoritative voices: ordained clergy, authors of books, university professors, newspaper journalists, foundation-based researchers, radio newsmen, and television anchors. Now, instead of a few voices of authority, there are many. Radio talk shows air everyone's truth. Television cameras get into the faces of bystanders at scenes of crime or natural disaster, allowing them to report what they saw and heard. Anyone may contribute an article to online encyclopedias. The age of United Methodism is an age when all persons are equal in defining the true and determining the newsworthy.

The last of the currents flowing out of the 1960s is *globalization*—freedom from limits imposed by national boundaries. At the moment of United Methodism's birth, Americans ate dinner watching the Vietnam War on television, with a time lag between battle fought and battle viewed. This lag vanished during the Iraq War: Americans watched the bombardment of Baghdad live. Four decades ago, Americans kept in touch with their loved ones in Vietnam by airmail letters. Now, over Internet connections, families use a webcam to see their loved ones in Iraq while typing instant messages into the same program. Then people came to church after a natural or human-made disaster, asking, "What can we do?" and their pastor answered, "I'll have a mailing from the United Methodist Committee on Relief by next Sunday." Now get-involved instructions pop up on pastors' computers within hours after an earthquake, massacre, or tsunami.

Globalization involves much more, however, than instantaneous communications across the globe—it involves such issues as free trade among nations, multinational corporations, international agreements to curb global warming, and interdependence of oil-drilling and oil-guzzling nations. For United Methodists, globalization means, in the words of the *Discipline*, that their distinctive theological heritage "is lived out in a global community, resulting in understandings of our faith enriched by indigenous experiences and manners of expression." This affirmation of "the contributions that United Methodists of varying ethnic, language, cultural, and national groups"[9] are making rests, in part, on the fact that a significant number of United Methodists do not live in the United States. Since 1995, overseas membership has grown by 68 percent, while the number of members in the United States has declined annually.

Globalization, like the other four currents on which United Methodism navigated after 1968, created eddies of disagreement. But a strong countercurrent rose about 1975—one that fought to reverse the flow of the cultural forces of the sixties. Historian Philip Jenkins calls it "Anti-Sixties" and describes the changed way of seeing the world associated with it. While the sixties generation saw societal problems and individual behavior as products of such forces as heredity, poverty, and social policy, the anti-sixties generation saw them in terms of right versus wrong—some nations and persons are simply evil, not dysfunctional. The United States and the Soviet Union were not two more of history's long line of great nations competing for resources and influence, as they were viewed in the 1960s. Rather, in anti-sixties rhetoric, a righteous America was in no-compromise conflict with an evil Soviet empire. In the post-9/11 era, it was *for-U.S.* or *against-U.S.* in the war on terrorism. This political rhetoric appropriated end-times imagery from Christianity, turning politics into no-holds-barred combat with the Antichrist, embodied in Osama bin Laden, Saddam Hussein, or "The Terrorist."

Jenkins reports that "of the multiple revolutions in progress by the early 1970s, perhaps the most sweeping involved gender roles and traditional notions of masculinity. Apart from the feminist upsurge, gay rights movements also offered startling challenges to older definitions of sex roles."[10] Responding, anti-sixties conservatives insisted that the husband is the head of the wife, that homosexual practices are sinful, and that "open homosexuality [in the military] is damaging to unit morale and cohesion."[11]

United Methodism's navigators never steered their church as far to the conservative right as American voters took the United States. Indeed, on some issues the church's official position was noticeably more liberal than that of the majority of American voters. For instance, in contrast with the laws of many states and a 1976 United States Supreme Court decision, the church opposed capital punishment, saying in its Social Principles: "We believe the death penalty denies the power of Christ to redeem, restore, and transform all human beings."[12]

Neither did Methodism knuckle under to populist homophobia. Alluding to the 1993 "don't ask, don't tell" law[13] that bars openly gay people from serving in the military, the 1996 General Conference called for including self-"outed" homosexuals in the armed forces: "The United States of America, a nation built on equal rights, has denied the right of homosexuals to actively serve their country while being honest about who they are. Meanwhile, the United Methodist Church is moving toward accepting all people for who they are. The United Methodist Church needs to be an advocate for equal civil rights for all marginalized groups, including homosexuals."[14]

While United Methodism steered more to the left on some issues, persistent pressure by the freshening wave of conservatism kept it somewhat center-right on its forty-year cruise on the currents of contemporary history. A log of its voyage follows.

Late Sixties

At the end of 1968, the year of United Methodism's birth, the United States launched *Apollo 8*, the first manned spacecraft to orbit the moon. The three astronauts jointly read the first ten verses of the book of

Genesis during a live Christmas Eve television broadcast. Before long, American atheist Madalyn Murray O'Hair filed suit against NASA for permitting the reading. Although the courts ultimately rejected her suit, it was a harbinger of the slugging matches between believers and nonbelievers, between biblical literalists and scientists, that would capture headlines in decades to come.[15] During the first full year of United Methodism's life, 1969, Neil Armstrong took "one small step for a man, one giant step for mankind" on the moon, *Sesame Street* debuted on Public Television, and United Methodism's men held their first national congress.

The Seventies

In 1970, the U.S. Department of Defense created a forerunner of the Internet, and a special General Conference, meeting in St. Louis, received progress reports from the commissions studying United Methodist doctrine, social principles, and church structure. Several women's organizations merged in 1971 to form the United Methodist Women. In the background, the success of the rock musical *Jesus Christ Superstar* signaled a turn toward religion in American popular culture. As the Watergate scandal, which led to the resignation of President Richard M. Nixon, began to grab headlines in 1972, General Conference met in Atlanta. It adopted the reports of the commissions dealing with United Methodist doctrine, structure, and social principles—adding to the latter the statement that the practice of homosexuality is "incompatible with Christian teaching."[16]

A 1973 Arab oil embargo sent gas prices soaring, and the stock market began a long plunge. In 1974, President Nixon, under threat of impeachment, resigned. The next year, 1975, Affirmation, a caucus supportive of full lay and clergy rights for gay men and lesbians, came into being on United Methodism's theological left; and Good News, a caucus on the right, issued the Junaluska Affirmation calling for identifying the core of United Methodist doctrine. At the same time, Bill Gates and Paul Allen founded Microsoft, and *Saturday Night Live* premiered.

As Americans observed the bicentennial of their Declaration of Independence in 1976, General Conference met in Portland, Oregon; for the first time, ten women served as clergy delegates. The Conference established the General Commission on the Status and Role of Women, prohibited the use of church funds to support gay or lesbian organizations, and refused to recognize same-sex marriage. In 1977, the testing of cell phones began, and United Methodist Renewal Services Fellowship brought together charismatics in the denomination. In 1978, John Paul II began a pontificate that moved Roman Catholicism toward the theological right. A 1979 revolution in Iran kicked out the U.S.-backed Shah, and Saddam Hussein grabbed power in Iraq. The United Methodist; African Methodist Episcopal; African Methodist Episcopal, Zion; and Christian Methodist Episcopal churches initiated Pan-Methodist dialogue, keeping in view the possibility of union.

When Jerry Falwell founded the Moral Majority in 1979, the tide of the Christian right was in full flow. The next year's election of President Ronald Reagan hoisted the banner of political conservatism over the White House. Clearly, by the end of the decade of the seventies, an anti-sixties current was surging through America's religious and political waters.

The Eighties

In 1980, Ted Turner launched Cable News Network, which soon called the attention of Americans to the Lech Walesa–led workers' strike in Gdansk, Poland. The 1980 General Conference, meeting in Indianapolis, created the General Commission on Christian Unity and Interreligious Concerns and rejected a proposal to ban self-avowed, practicing homosexual men and women from the ordained ministry. "Endless Love" by Diana Ross and Lionel Richie topped the charts in 1981, and Princess Diana and Prince Charles were honeymooning when, on August 12, IBM unveiled its 5150, precursor of the personal computer. Sony's Walkman, the first listen-as-you-jog stereo, appeared almost simultaneously. AIDS received its name in 1982, and Hezbollah arose as a radical Shiite Muslim party in Lebanon. United Methodism opened its new Archives and History Center in 1982 in Madison, New Jersey. In 1983, Sally Ride became the first American woman to travel in space, and the U.S. Congress set the third Monday in January as a holiday honoring Dr. Martin Luther King Jr. United Methodists busied themselves preparing to observe the bicentennial of American Methodism—a celebration that climaxed at the 1984 General Conference held in Baltimore.

Not only did the 1984 Conference remember two hundred years of American Methodist history, it also made history by setting up commissions to prepare a new hymnal and revise the 1972 doctrinal statement. This time, unlike 1980, delegates voted to ban self-avowed, practicing homosexual persons from the ordained ministry. Marking the increasing strength of the current of conservatism, persons on United Methodism's right launched their own Mission Society for United Methodists. What they objected to was expressed in 1969 by mission executive Tracey Jones, who predicted that missionary activity, instead of concentrating on saving persons from "a literal hell," would focus on liberating persons "from hunger, war, fear and human degradation" and increasingly confront "political and social power groups that take advantage of the weak."[17] The year 1985 stands out as the year Mikhail Gorbachev called for "openness" and "restructuring" in the U.S.S.R. The first Live Aid concert raised money for famine relief in Africa, scientists discovered a hole in the ozone layer over Antarctica, and United Methodist Hispanic women gathered for their first national convocation.

In 1986, United Methodism's bishops issued "In Defense of Creation," declaring: "We say a clear and unconditional *No* to nuclear war and to any use of nuclear weapons. We conclude that nuclear deterrence is a position that cannot receive the church's blessing."[18] This statement came in the wake of President Reagan's 1983 "Star Wars" proposal to defend the United States from missile attack and Soviet leader Yuri Andropov's counterthrust that "the United States, inspired by religious and apocalyptic ideas, was preparing a nuclear first strike on the USSR." This ramped-up rhetoric prompted atomic scientists to set the Doomsday Clock (a way of predicting the closeness of civilization to nuclear annihilation) at three minutes before midnight.[19] Also in 1986, Desmond Tutu was elected Anglican Archbishop of Cape Town, South Africa; the space shuttle *Challenger* exploded; and a nuclear accident at Chernobyl in the Ukraine killed 8,000 people. United Methodism marked a major publishing event in 1987 when it launched *Disciple*, a Bible-study program. That year also witnessed the first Palestinian Intifada ("uprising") against Israeli occupation of the West Bank and the Gaza Strip. Conservative United Methodists signed the Houston Declaration, which affirmed the primacy of Scripture, deplored "the effort ... to re-symbolize the Faith by abandoning the name of God, Father, Son, and Holy Spirit," and asserted that "the Church...has always considered homosexual practices as a sin."[20] On "Black Monday," October 19, 1987, the New York Stock

Market lost nearly a quarter of its value, leading to several years of financial belt-tightening for United Methodist congregations, conferences, and agencies.

United Methodism's *1988* General Conference adopted a revised doctrinal statement stressing the primacy of Scripture and retaining trinitarian God-language; approved a new, uniquely inclusive *Hymnal*; formed a committee to study homosexuality; voted to establish Africa University in Zimbabwe; and celebrated the centennial of the Deaconess movement in American Methodism. Other 1988 happenings include the terrorist-caused explosion of Pan Am Flight 103 over Lockerbie, Scotland; the election of President George H. W. Bush; and the formation of Hamas, a fundamentalist Islamic movement dedicated to the goal of making historic Palestine an Islamic state.

Two history-making developments punctuate the end of the eighties. The first was the fall of Communism in Europe. The second was the triumph of right-wing religion, ranging from sensitive conservatism to assertive fundamentalism. In *1989*, Pat Robertson put together the Christian Coalition, a fundamentalist political-action organization; and Iran's fundamentalist Muslim leader, Ayatollah Khomeini, mandated the death of Salman Rushdie, whose novel *Satanic Verses* suggested that Muhammad, not Allah, was the author of the Quran. The Communist government of East Germany resigned in 1989, precipitating the tearing down of the Berlin Wall. Also in 1989, the Communist governments of Bulgaria, Czechoslovakia, and Romania tumbled down, and free elections in the Soviet Union ousted the Communists. For United Methodists, 1989 saw the publication of their new *Hymnal*.

The Nineties

Iraq invaded Kuwait in *1990*, precipitating the next year the first American assault on Saddam Hussein's tyranny. Tim Berners-Lee and an associate assembled the components of what is now known as the World Wide Web. *The Simpsons* and *Seinfeld* premiered on television. And United Methodism's bishops called for "Vital Congregations—Faithful Disciples"[21] as a way to encourage church growth. In *1991*, President George H. W. Bush signed a civil rights act that strengthened existing laws and imposed penalties for intentional discrimination in employment. Four books rolled off the church's presses highlighting the historic contributions to United Methodism of Native Americans, Spanish-speakers, Asians, and African Americans.

The death certificate of the Cold War was signed by Russian president Boris Yeltsin and the first President Bush in 1992, while at the same time Osama bin Laden was setting al-Qaeda on foot. The 1992 General Conference, assembled in Louisville, authorized a new *Book of Worship* and received but did not endorse the report of the committee to study homosexuality. It did, however, "insist that all persons, regardless of age, gender, marital status, or sexual orientation, are entitled to have their human and civil rights ensured."[22] United Methodism's Africa University opened for classes in Old Mutare, Zimbabwe.

The first bombing of New York City's World Trade Center made headlines in 1993, while smaller type announced that Nokia had sent text messages between mobile phones. Many United Methodist women rejoiced in the liberation from oppressive male images of God—a liberation provided by the ecumenical Re-Imagining Conference held in Minneapolis in 1993; others reviled the gathering as pagan and supportive of goddess Sophia worship. In 1994, South Africans elected Nelson Mandela their first black president. Republicans, led by Newt Gingrich, won a majority in the House of Representatives, and then ushered in an anti-sixties agenda for America. United Methodists instituted a theological school in Tallinn, Estonia, with teaching in Estonian, Russian, and English.

Internet access became readily available in 1995; Amazon.com appeared on the Internet in July selling books; eBay opened for business; and a truck bomb destroyed a federal office building in Oklahoma City. United Methodist conservatives, meeting in Atlanta, ushered in the Confessing Movement, asserting the presence of a "crisis of faith within the United Methodist Church" and declaring: "We confess, in accordance with Holy Scripture and with the Holy Spirit's help, that Jesus Christ is the one and only Savior of the world."[23] Headlines in 1996 announced the birth of Dolly the sheep, the first mammal to be cloned; the election of Yasir Arafat as president of the Palestinian National Authority; the introduction of Google; and the first broadcast of Al Jazeera, an independent satellite station based in Qatar that revolutionized news dissemination in the Arab world.

The 1996 General Conference, held in Denver, adopted a theological statement, "By Water and the Spirit," dealing with baptism, and, breaking with two centuries of Methodist practice, reordered the church's ordained ministry, creating the orders of deacon and elder as separate and distinct offices. A statement was added to the *Discipline* prohibiting the celebration of same-sex unions in United Methodist churches, or anywhere by United Methodist clergy. In 1997, NASA's *Pathfinder* landed on Mars and sent back real-time images of the red planet, Britain's Princess Diana died in a car crash in Paris, and United Methodism's Board of Global Ministries inaugurated the Millennium Fund for Mission.

The U.S. House of Representatives voted in 1998 to impeach President William Clinton; the Senate acquitted him a year later. Also in 1998, Osama bin Laden proclaimed "holy war" against Jews and "Crusaders," Viagra received approval as the first oral drug to treat male impotence, and United Methodism's Judicial Council sustained the prohibition of same-sex ceremonies enacted by the 1996 General Conference. Homegrown terror captivated Americans in 1999, when shootings at Columbine High School in Colorado killed fourteen students and one teacher. Many around the planet worried that the so-called Y2K bug would wipe out computers on January 1, 2000. Others believed God had chosen the year 2000 as the time to wrap up the world. Worriers and believers alike awoke to a still spinning, increasingly computerized globe. United Methodist pastor Jimmy Creech lost his clergy credentials in 1999 for officiating at a same-sex covenant service,[24] and the Confessing Movement, a growing conservative group within United Methodism, presented its Indianapolis Affirmation, which rejected "efforts to extend to same-sex domestic partners those rights generally reserved to preserve and support heterosexual marriage."[25]

The New Millennium

In 2000, the world's population tipped over the six billion mark, of whom fewer than three hundred million lived in the United States. George W. Bush became President. Vermont provided civil unions for gay and lesbian couples. "Reality TV" mesmerized Americans, beginning with *Who Wants to Be a Millionaire?* and *Survivor.* And the 2000 General Conference, convened in Cleveland, sustained the church's position against rebaptism and infant dedication, and approved the publication of a Korean-English hymnal. In the midst of protests outside the convention center that resulted in the arrests of several bishops and a considerable number of clergy and laity, the Conference reiterated the denomination's view that same-sex practices are incompatible with Christian teaching. Delegates confessed the sin of racism in the church during a worship service.

September 11, *2001*, joined December 7, 1941, as "a date which will live in infamy." More than three thousand people died in attacks on the World Trade Center, the Pentagon, and a plane flying over Pennsylvania. President Bush, having identified Osama bin Laden and his al-Qaeda network as being responsible for the carnage, declared "War on Terror." Within weeks, U.S. and allied forces toppled the Afghanistan's Taliban regime, which was suspected of harboring Osama; he eluded capture. United Methodists issued *Come, Let Us Worship*, a Korean-English hymnal. In 2002, President Bush lumped together Iran, Iraq, and North Korea as an "axis of evil," and suggested the United States would preemptively strike states suspected of developing weapons of mass destruction. The Houston-based Enron Corporation declared bankruptcy, and SARS (Severe Acute Respiratory Syndrome) broke out in China. Roman Catholicism reverberated with accusations of sexual abuse by priests and cover-ups by bishops. United Methodism initiated dialogue with Episcopal Church leaders about mutual recognition of clergy, and started conversations with representatives of the Muslim Public Affairs Council.

In 2003, Methodists around the globe celebrated the three hundredth anniversary of John Wesley's birth. American and British troops invaded Iraq, quickly ending the rule of Saddam Hussein; before long, however, it became apparent that order and peace would not be quickly established. The space shuttle Columbia broke up on reentry. State laws imposing criminal penalties for same-sex practices were overturned by the U. S. Supreme Court.

In Iraq in 2004, Shiite and Sunni radicals savaged Americans and fellow Iraqis suspected of collaborating "with the occupiers." Mel Gibson's film *The Passion of the Christ* packed theaters in Lent. During a six-week period, four hurricanes struck Florida and nearby areas; later, just after Christmas, a gigantic earthquake off the coast of Sumatra raised a tsunami that left a quarter million people dead in coastal regions around the Indian Ocean. "This Holy Mystery," a theological statement of the meaning of the Lord's Supper in United Methodism, gained approval at the 2004 General Conference that met in Pittsburgh. "Being a self-avowed practicing homosexual"[26] was specified as a chargeable offense for which a clergy person could be tried in a church court. Expansion of the media campaign—"Open Hearts. Open Minds. Open Doors."—received approval. Later in 2004, a church trial in the Eastern Pennsylvania Conference found Irene Elizabeth ("Beth") Stroud guilty of being a "self-avowed practicing homosexual."

In 2005 United Methodists contributed $41.5 million to alleviate suffering caused by the late-December 2004 earthquake and tsunami in South Asia. Then, in early autumn, they gave another $24 million in response to Hurricane Katrina, which devastated parts of Mississippi, Louisiana, and Texas, and destroyed United Methodism's historic Gulfside Assembly in Mississippi. When Pope John Paul II died in 2005, he was succeeded by an equally if not more conservative theologian, Joseph Ratzinger, who took the papal name Benedict XVI. Although Iraqis voted in 2005 for a constitution and new leaders, anti-American violence intensified, as did Shiite versus Sunni terrorist acts. Gas prices topped three dollars a gallon. Liberians elected a president, Ellen Johnson-Sirleaf, a United Methodist; and the first United Methodist woman bishop outside the United States, Rosemarie Wenner, took office in the Germany Central Conference. The Judicial Council, United Methodism's highest court, sustained in 2005 the conviction of Irene Elizabeth ("Beth") Stroud on charges of being a "self-avowed practicing homosexual." The Council also ruled that the Virginia Conference acted incorrectly when it disciplined a pastor, Ed Johnson, for refusing to receive a gay man into his church's membership; the church's bishops, responding to the ruling, declared that homosexuality is not a barrier to membership.

2006—A Turning Tide?

In 2006, United Methodists celebrated the fiftieth anniversary of the General Conference decision that gave Methodist women full ordination rights, but the *New York Times* headlined reality: "Clergywomen Find Hard Path to Bigger Pulpit." The article, which featured several United Methodist clergywomen, observed that it may be easier to be elected bishop than to be selected to head a large congregation.[27] Also in 2006, the Board of Church and Society unveiled a proposed new Social Creed for United Methodism and invited musicians to set it to a variety of musical styles.

When a milk-truck driver killed five Amish schoolgirls and injured five others in early October 2006, television anchors and their viewers found

21

themselves dumbfounded in the presence of the Amish ethic of forgiveness. When "asked about the killings," one reporter wrote that the Amish "focused on forgiveness, faith and a determination to move forward."[28] The "world's second richest man," Warren Buffett, added $31 billion in 2006 to the Bill and Melinda Gates Foundation, which funds programs for combating HIV/AIDS and dealing with poverty around the world. Announcing his gift, Buffett observed that "American capitalism...has not worked in terms of poor people," and he "derided those made rich by inherited wealth as 'members of the lucky-sperm club.' "[29]

Perhaps the major event of 2006 was the marked change in how persons in the United States and across the planet viewed the American response to 9/11. Shortly after the attacks on the World Trade Center and the Pentagon, France's *Le Monde* newspaper proclaimed: "We are all Americans." Country music star Darryl Worley declared: "Some say this country's just out looking for a fight / After 9/11, man, I'd have to say that's right."[30] On March 10, 2003, as war in Iraq loomed, Natalie Maines, lead singer of the Dixie Chicks, told an audience in London that she was "ashamed" that Mr. Bush was from her home state of Texas.[31] Maines's sally caused the Chicks to lose half of their concert attendance in the United States, but when the Grammy Awards were announced early in 2007, they won all five categories for which they were nominated.[32] A line in a play by British playwright David Hare showcased the altered European assessment of the United States: "On September 11th, America changed. Yes. It got much stupider."[33] A September 11, 2006, editorial asserted that "Iraq, which had nothing to do with 9/11 when it was invaded, is now a breeding ground for a new generation of terrorists."[34] Later that month, a National Intelligence Estimate reported that the "Iraqi conflict has become the cause célèbre for jihadists, breeding a deep resentment of U.S. involvement in the Muslim world."[35] Then in the November 2006 elections, United States voters rejected their President's handling of the Iraq War, repudiated Republican Party right-wingers, and turned over control of the Senate and House of Representatives to Democrats.

The question is: Is the political and religious tide now flowing toward the left? The answer to this question is important for United Methodists. Their church has always tried to be centrist, or center-left, a position hard to hold after the late 1970s, when the tide of right-wing religion and politics freshened in the United States. If, however, the 2006 elections mark a reverse in that flow, then United Methodism's traditional position might be more tenable. And some observers detect such a reversal: "The religious right is in the doldrums. Last November, as the socially liberal Arnold Schwarzenegger stormed to re-election in California, social conservatives bombed. Rick Santorum barely scraped 40 percent of the vote in the Senate race for Pennsylvania, a dreadful result for a two-term senator. And conservatives lost a series of ballot initiatives—on abortion in South Dakota and California, stem-cell research in Missouri and gay marriage in Arizona."[36]

A number of books published in 2006—for example, *The God Delusion* by Richard Dawkins and *Letter to a Christian Nation* by Sam Harris— indict religion, especially irrational religion, on the charge of instigating bloodshed. These books that evangelize for atheism often mirror religious fundamentalism in their alarmist rhetoric. Their very extremism, however, may open space for a more rational presentation of Christianity, and United Methodists may be almost uniquely qualified to step into it; for a combination of reason and faith was favored by John Wesley who, anticipating Dawkins and Harris, said that "nothing has done more disservice to religion . . . than a sort of zeal which has . . . slain . . . its ten thousands."[37] Rejecting the savoring of bloodshed to which the irrational in all faith traditions seem prone, Wesley sought to create a "Vital Center"[38]—a Christian movement that would hold reason and religion, knowledge and piety in tension.

At Forty

If there is an incipient rebellion in American culture against right-wing religion and politics, then the celebration in 2008 of United Methodism's fortieth birthday may have something of the nature of a reprise; for the newborn United Methodist Church was a center-left denomination in 1968. Other aspects of the birthday party, too, may display a repeat-performance quality. Just as in 1968, the United States is engaged in a war from which a mounting number of its citizens suspect it will be forced to withdraw without achieving the administration's goals. Controversies about sexual practices continue to divide Americans as they did forty years ago. The unfinished United Methodist business, about which Professor Albert Outler spoke at the uniting conference, remains unfinished. Almost every General Conference reshapes one or more of the church's structures and ministries. And finally, although The

United Methodist Church is smaller in 2008 than it was in 1968, it remains a big denomination made up of small congregations.

The following chapters flesh out the overview just provided, telling the story of the United Methodist connection, its doctrine and theology, worship, ministry, mission, and social engagement.

For further reading, see Rex D. Matthews, *Timetables of History for Students of Methodism* (Nashville: Abingdon Press, 2007).

CHAPTER 3

CONNECTION

The editor of a local newspaper was challenged by a reader who was unhappy about the editor's position on religious matters. "I bet you don't belong to a church," the reader complained. The editor replied, "I'm not a member of any organized denomination. I'm a United Methodist." As the editor knows, United Methodism is highly organized—some say too much so. It is structured as a connection, "a vital web of interactive relationships"[1] that binds its members, churches, and conferences together for worship, nurture, and mission in the name of Christ. Yet, since its inception in 1968, United Methodist connectionalism has run headlong into a culture that has been ensnared by the individualism and localism described in the previous chapter.

United Methodist connectionalism originated with John Wesley. From the beginning Wesley referred to his scattered Methodist societies, bands, classes, and especially his preachers in eighteenth-century England as ministering in "connexion" with him. They were under his direction. By the final years of his life he spoke of Methodism as "the connexion" in a more formal sense as a pattern of Methodist theology, life, and organization, emphasizing the interdependence of its various parts.[2] It was a nurturing fellowship of preachers and people whose purpose was loving God and neighbor. American Methodists appropriated the term as early as their first annual conference in 1773 when they described themselves as laboring in America in "connexion with Mr. Wesley."[3] A term common to Methodism since its beginnings, connection remains a principal characteristic of United Methodism.[4]

Preparing for a New Connection

Formal and informal conversations between the Evangelical United Brethren Church (EUBC) and the Methodist Church (MC) took place during the 1950s seeking to determine a future relationship. The churches' deep historic ties, dating back to the eighteenth century, described in the introduction, and their twentieth-century ecumenical commitments created a growing desire to unite. In 1958 the EUBC General Conference authorized its Commission on Church Federation and Union to continue conversations with the Methodists "for the purpose of developing possible bases of consideration for union."[5] At its 1960 General Conference the MC approved the preparation of a plan of union and in 1964 received a favorable progress report from its Commission on Church Union. Meanwhile, the 1962 EUBC General Conference granted approval, by a 310 to 94 vote, to draft a plan of union, although concern was voiced about several organizational issues, including the racially segregated Methodist jurisdictional structure, the process of selecting conference (district) superintendents, and the tenure of bishops.

After securing approval from each denomination, the union commissions of both churches and their related committees met frequently from 1962 to 1966, their joint efforts culminating in the publication of a draft Plan of Union in April 1966. With the Plan document in hand the two churches' General Conference delegates assembled in November 1966 in separate meeting rooms of a Chicago hotel. Convening in the same location facilitated conversation between the two. For Evangelical United Brethren delegates it was the year of their regularly scheduled quadrennial General Conference, while for Methodists it was a special "adjourned" session of their 1964 General Conference.

After presentation and discussion of the Plan document a vote was taken separately by each General Conference. EUBC delegates approved the Plan by 325 votes to 88, only 16 votes more than the 75 percent needed to adopt it.[6] As provided in the EUBC *Discipline*, the Plan was then sent to the annual conferences where it was approved 3,740 to 1,607, just 174 votes more than the two-thirds necessary for ratification.[7] The Methodist vote was not close. General Conference delegates overwhelmingly adopted the union, 749 to 40, and it was ratified by its annual conferences 29,627 to 4,192.[8] Celebration of the union was set for April 23–May 4, 1968, in Dallas, Texas.

Connected by the Plan of Union

Great anticipation marked the meeting of the delegates of the two denominations in Dallas on April 23, 1968, to form The United Methodist Church (UMC). In the context of worship, EUBC Bishop Reuben H. Mueller and Methodist Bishop Lloyd C. Wicke together announced the union of the two denominations, "Lord of the Church, We are united in Thee, in Thy Church, And now in The United Methodist Church!" The declaration was greeted with a resounding congregational "Amen." Hope for the new life and ministry of the UMC church was affirmed by Methodist theologian and ecumenist Albert C. Outler in his Uniting Conference sermon, "Visions and Dreams," based on the description of Pentecost in Acts 2. Outler declared:

> We *must* find our way forward in conscious concern for the continuum of the Christian tradition and history in which we stand with our forefathers: always aware of God's habit of linking the past and the future by means of the hopeful acts of men in decisive *present* moments—like *this one!* We must learn to discipline our imaginations and inventions, not by our own constrictive biases, but by God's open-hearted mandates for his people, by patterns that will serve our *common* life in the Body of Christ.[9]

The Plan of Union by which the new church was initially organized consisted of two main parts: an opening nine-page "Historical Statement," which gave brief summaries of the histories of the EUBC and the MC, and the Constitution of the new church. The constitutional section was separated into five "Divisions" that dealt with content similar to the five divisions of the current United Methodist Constitution, although a number of changes in the constitutional text have been made since 1968.

The Plan announced the name of the new body, The United Methodist Church, a designation considered by the union commissions of both denominations as early as 1966. Paul A. Washburn, member of the EUBC Commission on Church Federation and Union, held that this denominational name was appropriate because it included evidence of the names of both uniting churches, "United" and "Methodist." He also argued that it clearly recognized that the union embraced a number of predecessor churches that had united over the past two centuries and that the name could easily be used for legal purposes in nations outside the United States where the EUBC and the MC had organized ministries.[10]

One of the principal concerns addressed in the Plan was the unequal size of the two churches. At union the MC was more than ten times the size of the EUBC. Therefore, the Plan specified a formula that would ensure that the EUBC, despite its smaller size, would have "effective representation" in the connectional life of the church for three quadrennia.[11]

Although it was decided to incorporate the Methodist jurisdictional system into the new denomination, its racial character was unsettling to many. Racial segregation was built into the structure of the MC when its jurisdictional system was created in the 1939 union. In addition to five regional jurisdictions composed of white annual conferences, Methodists established a racially segregated sixth jurisdiction, the Central Jurisdiction, in which were placed all of its African American annual conferences. Evangelical United Brethren and many Methodists were determined that the new church would not be structurally segregated by race. The Plan of Union not only asserted a policy of inclusiveness for membership and participation in the church's programs, it also effectively abolished the racially composed Central Jurisdiction. Article II of the Plan read that no jurisdictional conference shall be "based on any ground other than geographical and regional" factors.[12] The Plan provided for the continuation of the Methodist jurisdictional system with its five jurisdictions—North Central, Northeastern, South Central, Southeastern, and Western—and the states encompassed by each.[13] Following the designation employed before union by the Methodists, the groupings of annual conferences outside the United States were called central conferences rather than jurisdictional conferences.

The Plan of Union incorporated a number of provisions about ministry, superintendency, and episcopacy. These are examined in chapter 5.

Another important provision of the Plan dealt with judicial administration. Both churches had provisions in their *Disciplines* for dealing with judicial matters. Methodists utilized a denominational Judicial Council as a court of final decision on matters of church law and appeals. Methodism's Judicial Council was included in the Plan of Union.

Also employed in the Plan of Union was the term *connectional*,[14] a word very familiar to Methodists. Although the EUBC did not use the word in its *Discipline*, in fact it had been structurally connectional.

The 1968 Uniting Conference not only approved the Plan of Union, but also took other important actions, including the following:

- Established three quadrennial study commissions—Theological Study Commission on Doctrine and Doctrinal Standards, Social Principles Study Commission, and Structure Study Commission—and adopted the Methodist Commission on the Structure of Methodism Overseas.[15]
- Founded a Commission on Worship to consider revising existing orders of worship, preparing new orders, and supervising future editions of books of worship.[16]
- Created a Program Council to develop and coordinate the program emphases of the denomination.[17] The Program Council had been important to the ministry of the EUBC at the local church, annual conference, and general church levels.[18]
- Created a *Book of Resolutions*, placing miscellaneous resolutions related to social and other issues in a separate volume apart from its *Discipline*.[19]
- Formed a quadrennial Commission on Religion and Race (later a permanent general agency) and confirmed 1972 as the year to eliminate all forms of racial segregation in the structure of the new church.
- Merged the official men's groups of the former Evangelical United Brethren Men and Methodist Men into United Methodist Men, and the former denominational youth groups into the United Methodist Youth Fellowship. The women's groups were not joined until 1971.

Not all EUBC clergy and laity were convinced that the union was beneficial. They feared that their denomination would be swallowed up by the much larger Methodist body. The Plan of Union adopted by the Uniting Conference did not allay their fears since most of the Plan's provisions favored the Methodist way of doing things. While the EUBC insisted that the Central Jurisdiction be eliminated and their Program Council structure be adopted, Methodist practice prevailed on virtually all of the issues where there had been differences between the two denominations.

Some EUBC dissenters did not approve the Plan's provisions for the selection of bishops and superintendents. They were also concerned that Methodism was primarily committed to ecumenical relationships with other Wesleyan/Methodist bodies rather than the open ecumenism of the Evangelical United Brethren, which fostered connections with a more diverse group of denominations. Many questioned whether the Methodists were really able to deal with the Central Jurisdiction problem and the racism that supported it. Even before the union was consummated skeptical congregations in Montana and the Pacific Northwest petitioned in 1966 to withdraw from the EUBC. When their plea was denied and the union became a reality, the dissenters formed a new denomination, The Evangelical Church of North America, in June 1968.[20]

Structuring and Restructuring the Connection

The new church held a special session of its General Conference in St. Louis, Missouri, in April 1970 to check the pulse of the denomination and to make necessary adjustments. To the satisfaction of the delegates, progress reports were heard from the three commissions on theology, social issues, and structure. Final reporting of the commissions' labors was scheduled for the next General Conference in Atlanta, Georgia, April 1972.

Later chapters of this volume discuss the work of the theological and social principles commissions. Here we consider the final report of the Structure Study Commission whose task was "to study thoroughly the board and agency organizational structure of The United Methodist Church" and to recommend board and agency structuring for the new denomination.[21]

The structure commission reported that five principles guided its deliberations: effective program coordination, efficient organizational structure, accountability of denominational agencies, flexibility in deciding the church's missional priorities, and inclusive participation without regard to race or economic class. The design of United Methodism approved by the General Conference included three agencies for administration (Council of Bishops, Council on Ministries, Council on Finance and Administration), three service agencies (Board of Publication, Board of Pensions, Joint Committee on Communications), and four program agencies (Board of Church and Society, Board of Discipleship, Board of Higher Education and Ministry, Board of Global Ministries). Three commissions were also approved and later became permanent denominational agencies (Archives and History, Religion and Race, Status and Role of Women).

The forty-six-page structure document delineated the functions, responsibilities, and organization of the four program boards. The new boards consolidated the functions of a number of the predecessor denominations' agencies. For example, the new Board of Church and Society incorporated six former agencies of the EUBC and the MC, as well as United Methodism's Board of Christian Social Concerns.[22]

Replacing the Program Council created in 1968, a Council on Ministries was designated the chief coordinating body of the denominational program. Its task was to harmonize the ministry of the agencies to ensure the most effective use of staff and resources. Annual conference, district, and local church councils on ministries were also stipulated in the new structure.[23]

Ministries of denominational councils, boards, and commissions were supported by general funds of the church through apportionment giving of the local church.[24] The Council on Finance and Administration was empowered to recommend to the General Conference formulas assigned to each annual conference for its share of general funds apportionments.[25]

Local church structure in the new denomination mandated an elaborate organization that many congregations, especially the smaller ones, found difficult to implement. Each pastoral charge, which consisted of one or more local churches, was governed by a charge conference. Ministry of a local church, under pastoral leadership, was directed by an administrative board; a council on ministries; coordinators of children's, youth, adult, and family ministries; and other "work areas" appropriate to the local congregation. A woman's society and committees on nominations, pastor-parish relations, and finance were also prescribed.[26] Significant modifications in local church mandatory organization were made over the ensuing years. Heeding complaints of local churches about the burden of required organizational components, the 1980 General Conference enabled local churches to combine the work of the administrative board and the council on ministries into an administrative council.[27] Even more flexibility in the organization of the local church was adopted by the 1996 General Conference:

> The basic organizational plan for the local church shall include provision for the following units: a charge conference, a church council, a committee on pastor-parish relations, a board of trustees, a committee on finance, a committee on nominations and personnel, and such other elected leaders, commissions, councils, committees, and task forces as the charge conference may determine.[28]

Local church structure has changed little since 1996.

From the outset, like its predecessors, the prescribed annual conference structure of the new denomination was extensive. Each annual conference was required to have a Program Council (in 1972 named the Council on Ministries), as well as a Board of the Ministry, a Commission on World Service and Finance, a Committee on Interpretation, and several mandated boards, commissions, and committees.[29] Many of these were the annual conference counterpart of the denomination's general agencies.

Legislation of the 1996 General Conference not only simplified the required structure of the local church, but also allowed more flexible structure for the annual conference. The only mandated annual conference agencies were those dealing broadly with matters of ordained ministry and conference property. Without removing descriptions of necessary tasks and functions that were normally accomplished by conference agencies, each annual conference was given liberty to design ways in which it could fulfill these mandates. For example, whereas every annual conference was directed to have a conference commission on archives and history, it could employ an "alternative structure to provide for [the] functions [listed herewith] and maintain the connectional relationships."[30]

As the result of four years of research by the General Council on Ministries, the 1996 General Conference authorized a major study of the domestic and international structure of the denomination. The final report to the 2000 General Conference included a bold proposal to streamline the shape of the local church and annual conference.[31] Furthermore, it provided for a United States Central Conference replacing the jurisdictional conferences, retaining central conferences outside the United States, redesigning the work of the denomination's general agencies, and instituting a global council that would replace the denominational General Conference.[32] There was little enthusiasm for the proposed plan among denominational leaders and General Conference delegates even before the 2000 General Conference convened. The plan was finally rejected except for its final section titled "Living into the Future,"[33] which was referred back to the General Council on Ministries for study to be reported to the 2004 General Conference. Modifying subsequent recommendations from the General Council on Ministries, the 2004 General Conference replaced the General Council on Ministries, the effectiveness of which had been debated for several years, with the Connectional Table, a representative group of denominational leaders with no agency status and a very small staff, intended to coordinate, review, and evaluate the church's program agencies.[34]

Between 1972 and 2008 there were few other changes in the number of the denomination's general agencies. There are thirteen, including a council on finance; boards for pensions, publishing, discipleship, global ministries, higher education, and social issues; and commissions on racial matters, women, history, communications (added in 1976), ecumenical affairs (added in 1980), and men (added in 1996).

An Inclusive Connection

Since its birth in 1968 United Methodism has been committed to full membership, participation, and leadership of racial/ethnic persons and women in its ministry. Racial/ethnic and gender inclusiveness has been a denominational priority.

The Plan of Union specified that

> all persons without regard to race, color, national origin, or economic condition, shall be eligible to attend its worship services, to participate in its programs, and, when they take the appropriate vows, to be admitted into its membership in any local church in the connection. In The United Methodist Church no conference or other organizational unit of the Church shall be structured so as to exclude any member or any constituent body of the Church because of race, color, national origin, or economic condition.[35]

The dissolution of the Central Jurisdiction and the accompanying union of its former annual conferences and local churches with the other five jurisdictions was a resolute decision to erase structural segregation from the church. In 1964, four years prior to the union, three Central Jurisdiction annual conferences were united with annual conferences in other jurisdictions, and over the next nine years the remaining Central Jurisdiction conferences joined other jurisdictional conferences.[36]

Several other important developments solidified racial/ethnic inclusion in the church's life and leadership. A Commission on Religion and Race was formed in 1968 and remains a general agency whose purpose is to advocate inclusion and monitor the connection to ensure that racial/ethnic persons have full rights and equal participation in the whole life and mission of the church. Since 1972 every annual conference has been required to maintain a similar agency to guarantee racial/ethnic inclusiveness.

At the forefront of the denomination's commitment to racial/ethnic inclusion have been four caucuses. The first, Black Methodists for Church Renewal (BMCR), was formed in 1968. Its dramatic, peaceful protest at the Uniting Conference demonstrated the determination of blacks to participate fully in the total life of the new church.[37] The black caucus was a significant voice in founding the Commission on Religion and Race in 1968 and setting denominational priorities such as the $20 million Fund for Reconciliation (1968); the Ethnic Minority Local Church (1976–88), a plan devised in cooperation with other racial/ethnic caucuses to support racial/ethnic ministries; and Strengthening the Black Church for the 21st Century (1996–2008).

The Native American International Caucus (NAIC) traces its beginning to 1970. Advocacy, networking, identifying Native American leadership, sensitizing the church to Native American presence and needs, and strengthening Native American congregations have been its priorities. An important voice in the development of the Comprehensive Plan for Native American Ministries (1992–2008), the caucus continues to foster relationships between United Methodism and the Native American community.[38]

Methodists Associated Representing the Cause of Hispanic Americans (MARCHA) was founded in 1971. It has sought to provide fellowship and support for United Methodist witness and ministry among the growing Hispanic population in the United States. Vigorously supported by the caucus, the National Plan for Hispanic/Latino Ministry (1992–2008) launched a dynamic program to expand the number of Hispanic churches and cultivate leadership.[39]

Asian American United Methodists formally inaugurated the National Federation of Asian American United Methodists (NFAAUM) in 1974.[40] Bishop Wilber W. Y. Choy, the first Asian elected to the United Methodist episcopacy, described the mission of the National Federation:

> To articulate the concerns, interests and needs of the Asian American constituencies in all Jurisdictions of the Church;...to advocate the causes of Asian Americans before appropriate boards and agencies of the Church;...to promote relevant and meaningful Asian American ministries at all levels of the church; and...to encourage full participation of Asian Americans in all aspects of the life of the Church.[41]

Similar sentiments could have been spoken by the leaders of the other racial/ethnic caucuses.

Though not officially incorporated into the structure of the denomination, the caucuses have actively influenced denominational life and ministry. Many of their members have served on denominational boards and agencies, occupied influential pastorates, and effectively served as district superintendents, as bishops, and in other positions. Korean United Methodist leaders have been important in two of the denomination's ministry initiatives, the United Methodist Council on Korean American Ministries (2000–2008) and the Asian American Language Ministry Plan (2004–2008).

The Plan of Union did not specifically mention the matter of gender inclusiveness. It is clear, however, that women were not afforded equal opportunities in the life and leadership of the predecessor churches. A United Methodist Women's Caucus was formed in 1971. According to Thelma Stevens, longtime leader and spokesperson for the Methodist (later United Methodist) Woman's Division, the caucus's purpose was to provide a supportive fellowship for women, to effect change and justice, and to influence legislation at the 1972 General Conference.[42] One goal of the caucus was realized when the conference created the Commission on the Status and Role of Women, whose mission included advocacy for the full inclusion of women in the life of the church and monitoring to ensure that such participation occurred. Since 1976 annual conferences have been required to maintain a means to assure the full participation of women in their life.

Women's leadership in the connection has increased considerably over the years since union. Their commitment and talents have not only been visible in choirs, preparing and serving church suppers, and teaching Sunday school, but also increasingly as clergy; members and chairs of local church, district, annual conference, and general church boards and committees; annual conference lay leaders; and General Conference delegates. At the 1972 General Conference, about 13 percent of the delegates were women. In 2004 approximately 40 percent were women, including 34 percent of the clergy delegates.[43]

Race and gender have not been the only areas of inclusiveness with which the church has grappled. Caucuses have been formed by groups who have been intent on having their voices heard and influencing denominational life on a multitude of issues. The Methodist Federation for Social Action, founded as the Methodist Federation for Social Service in 1907, has lobbied the connection on a variety of social issues, including a change in the denomination's position on homosexuality.[44] Good

News, a caucus formed in 1967, has sought to voice the concerns and views of the denomination's evangelicals.[45]

There are eighteen caucuses and thirty-eight affiliated groups in the UMC.[46] Among those most active are Affirmation, a gay and lesbian caucus begun in 1975, and Aldersgate Renewal Ministries, with origins in 1977, organized to encourage United Methodists to be filled with the Holy Spirit and to employ the Spirit's gifts for ministry in the world. Other active caucuses and groups in the UMC seek to bring concerns and issues to the forefront of the denomination's consciousness, especially at the time and place of the General Conference. Although some have believed that these groups injure the unity of the denomination, each of them has been a catalyst forcing the church to deal with critical issues in its life and ministry.[47]

Connectional Communication

Recent decades have witnessed stunning changes in the ways people communicate with one another. Realizing that communicating with its constituency is critical to the life of the connection, the UMC, without abandoning traditional means of communicating, has endeavored to keep pace with new developments. Since union the denomination's communications program has been led by its General Commission on Communication (better known as United Methodist Communications), which became a denominational agency in 1976.

The printed word has been, and continues to be, the primary means of disseminating information to the membership. Weekly local church bulletins and monthly newsletters have informed congregations about programs and meetings. They have carried prayer lists and notices regarding the church's life and ministry.

Annual conferences have employed some sort of publication to communicate with laity and clergy. Beginning in the 1980s *The United Methodist Reporter*, a Texas-based independent weekly newspaper, gained wide circulation in some annual conferences. Although not an official denominational periodical, it posted denominational news and provided space in each issue, through contractual arrangement, for an annual conference to inform its constituency. While some conferences continued to use the *Reporter* as their principal publication, dwindling conference finances and the *Reporter's* controversial stance on denominational issues led some annual conferences to establish other means of communicating with their membership.

Denominational periodicals have continued to tell the story of the church's people and ministry as successors to magazines and publications of the predecessor denominations. The EUBC *Telescope Messenger* was superseded by *Church and Home*, which ceased publication in 1969 in favor of the colorful Methodist magazine *Together*, which by 1960 had a circulation of approximately one million and continued until 1973 when rising costs and declining interest in its format and content led to its demise. The official Methodist clergy publication *Christian Advocate*, which contained articles on the practice of ministry, was adopted by the new denomination until it was succeeded in 1976 by *Circuit Rider*. The Methodist quarterly journal, *Religion in Life*, became the denomination's quarterly theological journal until it was replaced in 1980 by *Quarterly Review*, which, for funding reasons and lack of subscribers, was terminated in 2005.

Since 1968 programming information for local church leaders has been provided by the denomination's *Interpreter* magazine. *El Interprete* has been its Spanish-language counterpart. United Methodist women have been provided with *Response*, successor to *The Methodist Woman* and the EUBC women's publication, *The World Evangel*.

The denomination's general agencies have published an abundance of newsletters, periodicals, and devotional resources for the church. Among them are the missions magazine *New World Outlook*; *The Upper Room* devotional guide; *Methodist History*; and *Newscope*, a weekly denominational newsletter. Caucuses and other unofficial denominational groups have contributed to United Methodist news and program literature through regular publications, two of which are *Social Questions Bulletin* (Methodist Federation for Social Action) and *Good News* (Good News).

Radio, television, film, and video proved to be useful media employed by the denomination to tell its story. Although some media programming initiative has been undertaken by local churches, denominational ministry in this area has been directed by United Methodist Communications, including the Igniting Ministries program adopted by the 2000 General Conference and renewed in 2004. Using television, newspaper, billboard advertising, and other media, Igniting Ministries seeks to raise public awareness about The United Methodist Church, inspire its membership, reach out to others seeking answers to life's deeper questions, and encourage the unchurched to visit a local congregation. "Open Hearts. Open Minds. Open Doors." was adopted as the campaign theme.

Computers, the World Wide Web, e-mail, blogs, Google, e-Bay, iPods, and other innovations have changed forever the way in which United Methodists gain information, enjoy music, and communicate with one another. Local churches, annual conferences, and denominational agencies began to utilize these means effectively in the 1990s. Denominational news can now be broadcast instantaneously. Every general agency of the church developed a website to describe its work, to announce new resources for spiritual growth and ministry, and to offer direct assistance to local churches and annual conferences. Although some church members did not have access to these new means of communicating, for those who did, it became easier for them to keep informed.

United Methodist presence is often signified by the "cross and flame," the official emblem or logo of the denomination. Highway and street signs display it. Local churches, annual conferences, and general agencies use it on publications, stationery, and name cards. It is found on banners and T-shirts, choir and clergy stoles, signboards and advertisements.

Whereas Methodists never chose a denominational emblem, in 1958 the Evangelical United Brethren adopted a circular emblem that pictured a Latin cross surrounded by the name of the church with clasped hands in the foreground representing the 1946 union of the Evangelical Church and the Church of the United Brethren in Christ.

Authorized by the 1968 UMC Uniting Conference, the new church's Program Council decided on the cross and flame to symbolize the denomination visually. Representing the sacrificial death of Jesus, they chose the cross, the most familiar symbol in the Christian faith. Recalling the description of Pentecost (Acts 2), the flame symbolizes the presence of the Holy Spirit in the church.[48]

The UMC logo is the official denominational emblem. It is used not only in the United States but also in other nations. United Methodist churches in Africa, Europe, and the Philippines use it to advertise the presence and ministry of their congregations.

Connectional Mathematics

Statistics may not be the most revealing information about the strength and effectiveness of a church, but they are an indication of its health and vitality. Historically, both the MC and the EUBC kept accurate statistical records of their churches.

Assessing denominational statistics since 1968 lays bare both distressing and hopeful news. Numbers for United Methodism in the United States show a steady decline in most important statistical categories. In 1967, the year before the union, the churches reported a total membership of 11,026,976 (EUBC: 737,762; MC: 10,289,214) in 41,993 local churches (EUBC: 3,933; MC: 38,060). Sunday church schools enrolled 7,086,158 (EUBC: 576,765; MC: 6,509,393). Total clergy were 32,890 (EUBC: 3,683; MC: 29,207). After union, in 1968 the UMC reported a fall in each of these categories. Membership in 1969 fell to 10,990,720; local churches to 41,901; clergy to 33,236; and Sunday church school enrollment to 6,852,285.[49] It is important to note, however, that declines in membership actually began in both churches before union.

As the accompanying table (Statistical Review) shows, every quadrennium in the United States since union has been marked by decline in church membership, average attendance at the principal Sunday worship service(s), church school membership and average attendance, and number of local churches. Between 1968 and 2003 membership fell 26 percent and church school enrollment declined 48 percent. While church school attendance decreased a sizable 56 percent for the same period, worship attendance fell only 14 percent. Unofficial figures for 2005 show membership at 7,995,429, down more than 1.7 percent over 2004;

attendance at 3,344,318, down more than 1.6 percent; and church school attendance down by more than 6 percent.[50] We regret that more recent official statistics were not available at the time of this writing.

Statistical Review for the United Methodist Church in the United States, 1969–2004[51]

Year	Church Membership	Average Worship Attendance	Church School Membership	Average Church School Attendance	Total Giving	Total Property Value
1969	10,754,973	3,991,877	6,251,642	3,464,689	$ 685,751,378	$ 5,499,348,929
1972	10,334,531	3,699,172	5,380,147	2,986,134	$ 833,916,494	$ 6,255,075,674
1976	9,749,753	3,617,671	4,521,992	2,335,031	$1,162,828,991	$ 9,154,194,212
1980	9,519,407	3,587,175	4,201,400	2,151,977	$1,632,204,336	$12,589,798,037
1984	9,229,370	3,549,347	4,020,661	2,033,871	$2,211,306,198	$18,384,191,232
1988	8,940,836	3,421,642	3,873,684	1,940,291	$2,697,918,285	$23,251,062,608
1992	8,688,472	3,453,465	3,835,113	1,867,874	$3,202,700,721	$27,878,716,470
1996	8,456,968	3,450,362	3,705,863	1,727,568	$3,744,692,223	$32,711,654,225
2000	8,296,836	3,487,629	3,590,824	1,591,646	$4,761,148,280	$39,636,992,168
2004	8,137,764	3,400,291	3,528,760	1,506,130	$5,541,538,286	$47,828,786,557

Another unwelcome statistic reveals that in 1970 United Methodists in the United States were approximately 5.2 percent of the population and by 2001 they were slightly below 3 percent. Membership of the predecessor denominations as a percentage of the United States population reached its peak in 1930 at 6.5 percent and has been falling ever since.[52] On a positive note, total giving and the total value of local church property and assets, not adjusted for inflation, rose dramatically from 1968 to 2004.

While the steady decrease in membership, church school enrollment, and numbers of local churches over the life of United Methodism in the United States is discouraging, similar statistics for the central conferences are heartening. In 1984 the central conferences reported 433,123 church members, 241,086 church school enrollees, and 4,224 local churches. By 2004 church membership had climbed to 3,497,512, church school enroll-ment to 599,963, and local churches to 6,934. Africa led the way in mem-bership with 3,227,162, followed by the Philippines with 201,309, and Europe with 69,041.[53] Africa's membership figure increased dramatically when the Protestant Methodist Church of Côte d'Ivoire united with the UMC in 2004, bringing 678,000 people into the United Methodist fold.[54]

Growth of the central conferences in Africa and the Philippines give those areas more voice and vote in the denomination's General Conference. Likewise, the shift of membership in the United States from the North Central, Northeastern, and Western jurisdictions to the South Central and Southeastern jurisdictions has given southern United Methodists more General Conference delegates and, therefore, a larger role in determining the program and ministry of the denomination.[55]

Downturns in membership and attendance in the United States have caused alarm in the denomination. Over the years analysts have offered multiple explanations.[56] Some are cultural, including an aggressive secularism that attempts to push God and church more and more into the background of life. Others are related directly to church life—lack of evangelism, inhospitable and parochial congregations, insufficient engagement with social issues, weak lay and clergy leadership, mournful worship, and passionless preaching, to name a few.

Whereas United Methodist membership and attendance statistics in the United States are troubling, denominational finances have not been as disturbing. Total giving, unadjusted for inflation, has increased in every quadrennium. Many local churches, however, have experienced the financial pinch of fewer contributors, increasing costs for property maintenance, higher salaries and insurance benefits, and higher apportionment askings from the annual conference and general church for support of ministries beyond the local church.[57] Believing that local ministry is a matter of first importance, and that apportionments maintain a distant and ineffective bureaucracy, many congregations have been tempted to lower their giving for denominational ministries, thereby threatening to suffocate connectional support.

Global Connection

Each of the uniting churches developed means by which it organized its denominational ministry outside the United States. Evangelical United Brethren work was under the direction of its Division of World Mission. Methodists organized their annual conferences into regional groups called central conferences.

The Methodist system of central conferences was maintained in the Plan of Union and became part of the United Methodist structure. Central conferences were entitled to all of the privileges granted them by the General Conference, including the election of bishops, determining annual conference boundaries, and adapting the denomination's *Discipline* to conditions within their boundaries except for matters that were reserved to the General Conference.[58] Virtually no change has been made in these provisions since union.[59] Prior to union there were ten Methodist central conferences located in three geographical areas: Africa, Asia, and Europe.[60] By 2004, due to consolidation, the number was seven, although there were more members and annual conferences, accelerated by growth in Africa and the Philippines.[61] Numerical growth in Africa and the Philippines translates into their greater influence in shaping some areas of the denomination's life. In 1992 the central conferences sent 116 delegates to the General Conference. The number increased to 188 at the 2004 General Conference, which accounted for 19 percent of the delegate total.[62]

Recognizing changing social circumstances of Methodists in other nations and a growing desire for self-determination and autonomy in those areas, in 1948 Methodists created a Commission on the Structure of Methodism Overseas, commonly known by its acronymn COSMOS.[63] Both COSMOS and the provision for central conferences were incorporated into the United Methodist connectional structure, although COSMOS was replaced in 1972 by a Committee on Central Conference Affairs.

The purpose of the Committee on Central Conference Affairs is similar to that of its predecessor and has not substantially changed over the years following its organization. The 1968 United Methodist *Book of Discipline* describes its work as follows: "Recognizing the differences in conditions that exist in various areas of the world and the changes taking place in those areas, there shall be a Commission on Central Conference Affairs to study the structure and supervision of The United Methodist Church in its work outside the United States and its territories and its relationships to other Church bodies." All resolutions, petitions, and recommendations related to the central conferences are considered by the commission before submission to the General Conference.[64] Among its responsibilities are examining proposals for autonomy submitted by United Methodist conferences and recommending action to the General Conference.

Ecumenical Connection

One of the hallmarks of twentieth-century Christianity is the ecumenical movement that brought Christian denominations into closer fellowship, cooperation, and, in some cases, actual union with one another. The Methodist/Evangelical United Brethren union was a consequence of this ecumenical spirit.

At the outset the Plan of Union stated the new church's commitment to relationships with other Christian churches:

> As part of the Church Universal, The United Methodist Church believes that the Lord of the Church is calling Christians everywhere to strive toward unity, and therefore it will seek, and work for, unity at all levels of church life: through world relationships with other Methodist churches and united churches related to The Methodist Church or The Evangelical United Brethren Church, through councils of churches, and through plans of union with churches of Methodist or other denominational traditions.[65]

Both predecessor denominations had strong ecumenical allegiances. They were early and passionate supporters of the National Council of Churches of Christ in the U.S.A., founded in 1950 as the successor to the Federal Council of Churches, and the World Council of Churches, formed in 1948. At various times leaders of both denominations provided top executive leadership for both councils.[66] A fear expressed by some EUBC members before union was that Methodists did not maintain the same levels of commitment to a broader ecumenism that included churches beyond the Wesleyan/Methodist family.[67] Methodists argued that they were firm advocates of ecumenism on every front—world, national, state, and local. Whatever the difference in perception, it is clear that from its origin United Methodism has not wavered in its commitment to the larger Body of Christ in the world. Through its representatives and funding it has supported both the national and world councils.

When the UMC was formed in 1968 its structure included a Commission on Ecumenical Affairs, one of its general agencies, which was "to proclaim and work for the unity of the Church."[68] Four years later this body lost agency status when it was organized as a division of the General Board of Global Ministries. Ecumenical interests were again accorded general agency status in 1980 when the General Conference established the General Commission on Christian Unity and Interreligious Concerns whose task, as its name suggests, is not only to guide the denomination's relationships with other Christian churches but also with other world faiths.

Linking the family of churches that trace their origins to the eighteenth-century Wesleyan movement is the principal task of the World Methodist Council. Organized in 1881, the council links the wider family of approximately 39 million Methodists in more than 130 countries. United Methodism represents the largest denominational membership among these churches and has historically furnished both leadership and substantial funding for its work.[69]

The four largest Methodist denominations in the United States have been divided since the nineteenth century along racial lines. In addition to the UMC they include the African Methodist Episcopal Church, the African Methodist Episcopal Zion Church, and the Christian Methodist Episcopal Church. The Episcopal Address at the 1968 Uniting Conference voiced a fervent desire to achieve a reunion of these four churches since they share common historic roots and mission.[70] Joint efforts resulted in a Commission on Pan-Methodist Cooperation in 1985 and a Commission on Union in 1996. Four years later a Commission on Pan-Methodist Cooperation and Union replaced the earlier commissions and a fifth church, the Union American Methodist Episcopal Church, joined. The commission's mission is to heal the wounds of past divisions in order to offer the world a more effective witness and more efficient use of denominational resources.[71] Since 2000, voting representatives of Pan-Methodist denominations serve on the general agencies of the UMC, a sign of United Methodism's desire to engage more fully with Pan-Methodist churches.[72] A moving service of repentance and reconciliation for the circumstances that caused major racial divisions among American Methodists was held at the 2000 General Conference, accompanied by symbolic wearing of sackcloth and ashes. Pan-Methodist leaders were present and participated in the liturgy. Not overlooking the importance of African Americans who remained in the UMC and its predecessors, a service of thanksgiving and appreciation for their historic role in the denomination was held at the 2004 General Conference.

Concordat agreements have been established by the UMC with other churches. Approved by the General Conference, these formal agreements provide for mutual visitations by United Methodist bishops and their counterparts in the concordat churches as well as the possible transfer of clergy between concordat churches and the UMC.[73] Among those with whom such agreements exist are the Methodist Church of Mexico, the Methodist Church in the Caribbean and the Americas, the Methodist Church of Puerto Rico, and the Methodist Church in Great Britain.[74]

Participation in ecumenical conversations and dialogues with Eastern Orthodox, Roman Catholics, Episcopalians, Reformed, and Lutherans have also proved to be important means of ecumenical relationship.[75] We cannot conclude this section without reference to Churches Uniting in Christ, the 2002 successor to the Consultation on Church Union, which was founded in 1962 and in which the MC and EUBC were two of the original ten members. One of nine members of the Churches Uniting in Christ, the UMC has joined in covenant with other members to practice regular sharing of the Lord's Supper, to join in the common evangelical and prophetic mission of God, and to combat racism. United Methodist support for Churches Uniting in Christ is another evidence of ecumenical commitment.

Connection at Forty

Since 1988 every edition of *The Book of Discipline of The United Methodist Church* has described the life and ministry of the UMC as "The Journey of a Connectional People."[76] United Methodism has been, and continues to be, on a journey. During its pilgrimage the connection has paused to celebrate facets of its history. In 1984 it observed the bicentennial of the formation of the Methodist Episcopal Church, its parent body in North America. With the theme "Proclaiming Grace and Freedom," local churches, annual conferences, and the General Conference remembered their Methodist roots. In 2003 and 2007 the three-hundredth birthdays of John and Charles Wesley respectively, Methodist founders were recalled with appropriate publications, drama, and musical celebrations. In 2008 it commemorates the bicentennial of the death of Jacob Albright, founder of the Evangelical Association. With the rich diversity of United Methodism's history, almost every year produces an opportunity for some sort of historical festivity.

United Methodism has organized its life and ministry and reshaped its connectional structure to meet challenges in various places around the globe. Racial/ethnic persons and women have increasingly contributed talent and leadership to the life of the denomination on a scale never previously witnessed. Although membership and attendances have fallen in the United States, United Methodists have continued to open their wallets and pocketbooks to support the work of the local church and the larger connection. The denomination has rejoiced in its substantial growth in the Philippines and Africa. From the outset it has understood itself as a full participant in the larger Body of Christ.

Whereas many United Methodists may recognize the importance of denominational connectionalism with its vast resources and ministries, many United Methodists have no idea about what it means to be a connectional church or the opportunities and blessings connectionalism affords. As mentioned in the first chapter, individualism, localism, and theological and social polarization threaten to erode the connection and its potential for ministry. At the 1980 General Conference in Indianapolis, a hotel that housed some delegates posted on its large outdoor signboard a greeting in bold letters for everyone passing to see: WELCOME UNTIED METHODISTS. The following chapters explore some of the critical issues that will determine whether the denomination is, and will be, untied or united.

For further reading, see Thomas Edward Frank, *Polity, Practice, and the Mission of The United Methodist Church* (Nashville: Abingdon Press, 2006), and Russell E. Richey, Dennis M. Campbell, and William B. Lawrence, eds., *Connectionalism: Ecclesiology, Mission and Identity*, vol. 1 of *United Methodism and American Culture* (Nashville: Abingdon Press, 1997).

CHAPTER 4

DOCTRINE AND THEOLOGY

The United Methodist Church began life at a time, the late 1960s, when newcomers were unlocking the doors of theology's house, moving in, and repainting the walls. Among these decorators were proponents of various *protesting* theologies—"black theology, female liberation theology, political and ethnic theologies, third-world theology, and theologies of human rights."[1] This openness to fresh and bright theological colors found expression in positive references to doctrinal and theological *pluralism*.[2] Responding to these many-colored theologies, United Methodist traditionalists called for naming the black-and-white essentials of Christian doctrine. Sometimes the traditionalists borrowed the five fundamentals of Fundamentalism; sometimes they stuck with the "main doctrines" of John Wesley—repentance, faith, and holiness.[3]

Wesley's writings gained, very slowly, the attention of researchers during the two decades before United Methodism's birth. Then came articles and books by Wesley scholars, whose successes prompted the Oxford University Press to take on a Wesley Works Project, floating it in 1975 with the publication of Wesley's *Appeals to Men of Reason and Religion*—an apt choice because the Wesleyan tradition tries to hold precise thinking and passionate believing in creative tension. United Methodism's Abingdon Press took over the Wesley Works Project and issued the first volume of Wesley's *Sermons* as part of the 1984 celebration of American Methodism's bicentennial.

Probably more preachers read the church-growth theories of United Methodist sociologist Lyle Schaller, whose Abingdon Press books sold well over a million copies,[4] than studied the spiritual-formation theology of John Wesley. But most of the credit for the theological formation of

United Methodist clergy goes to an array of less well-selling scholars who approach God and Jesus from evangelical, liberationist, feminist, orthodox, environmental, and various racial/ethnic points of view. Two series significantly shaped lay theological thought: the United Methodist Publishing House's DISCIPLE: *Becoming Disciples Through Bible Study,* a program launched in 1987, which, by the late 1990s, was used in more than ten thousand churches;[5] and the study books commissioned annually by the United Methodist Women dealing with themes such as "John Wesley: Holiness of Heart and Life."

Adding Color to Theology's Walls: Restoring Black and White

New scarlets and golds brightened Protestantism's traditionally black-and-white theology during the 1960s. Methodist and Evangelical United Brethren worship leaders studied the liturgical documents of the Roman Catholic Church's Vatican Council II (1962–65). Jewish sage Martin Buber's *I and Thou* changed the way many clergy presented the human-God interrelationship. Systematic theologian Carl Michalson introduced his fellow Methodists to the theology of the pain of God articulated by Japanese theologian Kazoh Kitamori.[6] Thomas Altizer, a religion professor at Methodist-related Emory University, headlined "Death of God" theology. And African Methodist Episcopal theologian James H. Cone released *Black Theology and Black Power* in 1969.

The book that jolted American pew-sitters was *Honest to God* (1963) by Church of England bishop John A. T. Robinson. Robinson taught laypersons Paul Tillich's idea that God is not a Being superior to all other beings, but rather the *Ground* of all being. Also Robinson presented Rudolf Bultmann's program of removing such "myths" as the incarnation and ascension from the Gospels. For many reared on checklists of moral dos and don'ts, Robinson brightened the landscape, saying: "Nothing can of itself be labeled as 'wrong.'... The only intrinsic evil is lack of love."[7]

For doubters searching for belief it was bliss to be alive in the sixties, but for staunch believers it was a decade of spiritual queasiness. Methodist pastor Charles Keysor spoke for the latter when he published an article in 1966 in the church's *Christian Advocate* titled "Methodism's Silent Minority." Keysor wrote: "I speak of those Methodists who are variously called 'evangelicals' or 'conservatives' or 'fundamentalists.' A more accurate description is 'orthodox,' for these brethren hold a traditional under-standing of the Christian faith."[8]

In the midst of this conflict between those trying on new Joseph's coats of theology and those keeping their old black-and-white cloaks, the newly formed United Methodist Church approached the task of defining its doctrine.

The 1968 Plan of Union

The plan that guided the Methodist and Evangelical United Brethren union placed the two churches' doctrinal statements—the Methodist Articles of Religion and the Evangelical United Brethren Confession of Faith—side by side and declared them "congruent if not identical in their doctrinal perspectives and not in conflict."[9] John Wesley selected Methodism's Articles in the eighteenth century, when they were already two hundred years old, having been written in the mid-sixteenth century for the newly formed Church of England, which was engaged in fierce conflict with Roman Catholicism over questions of doctrine and practice. Wesley chose twenty-four of the original thirty-nine Articles and handed them on to American Methodists in 1784. The 1808 General Conference adopted a rule that made it all but impossible to "revoke, alter, or change" the Articles that Wesley picked.[10] The Evangelicals and United Brethren, on the other hand, revised their statements of faith during the century and a half they existed as separate churches, and after their merger in 1946 they drafted a new Confession of Faith that was adopted in 1962.

Recognizing that there were differences between the Articles of Religion and Confession of Faith, as well as archaic language and dated doctrinal issues in the Methodist Articles, members of the uniting con-ference established a commission to study the problem and report to the 1972 General Conference. The commission's mandate allowed it to pre-pare "a contemporary formulation of doctrine and belief."[11]

Theological Study Commission, 1968–72

Commission members decided, first, that it was inadvisable to draft a new statement of faith. There were too many discordant colors in late-sixties' theologizing to make harmonization possible. Instead, guided by their chairman, Wesley authority Albert Outler, they drafted a new section for the *Discipline*—"Doctrine and Doctrinal Statements and the General Rules,"[12] which was adopted 925 to 17 by the 1972 General Conference.[13] Embedded in this section are the Articles of Religion, the Confession of Faith, and John Wesley's General Rules for his followers,[14] all of which are protected from easy alteration by United Methodism's Constitution.[15] However, they "are *not* to be regarded," the *Discipline* stipulated, as doctrinal statements "demanding unqualified assent," but rather "as important landmarks in our complex heritage" of doctrinal and theological reflection.[16]

Central to the fresh material in the 1972 *Discipline* is the Quadrilateral. "By what methods," the *Discipline* asks, "can our doctrinal reflection and construction be most fruitful and fulfilling? The answer comes in terms of free inquiry within the boundaries defined by four main sources and guidelines for Christian theology: Scripture, tradition, experience, reason."[17] Of these, "Scripture is the primary source and guideline,"[18] but all four are "interdependent.... They allow for, indeed they positively encourage, variety in United Methodist theologizing."[19]

Underlying the presentation of the Quadrilateral in the 1972 *Discipline* were three decisive factors in United Methodism's theological situation: pluralism, protesting theologies, and historical consciousness. In Outler's words, there always is somebody in United Methodism "urging every kind of theology still alive and not a few that are dead."[20] This theological pluralism, according to the 1972 *Discipline*, "should be recognized as a principle"[21]—a limited one, however, because United Methodist theologizing draws its blood cells from "a 'marrow' of Christian truth," which "stands revealed in Scripture, illumined by tradition, vivified in personal experience, and confirmed by reason."[22] The elements of this marrow are identified as affirming "the triune God," "the mystery of salvation in and through Jesus Christ," and the way the Holy Spirit "enables us to accept God's gift of reconciliation and justification."[23]

The principle of pluralism, understanding that "all truth is from God," affirms "efforts to discern the connections between revelation and reason, faith and science, grace and nature."[24] In addition, because "God has been and is now working among all people," truth is to be discovered through "interfaith encounters and explorations between Christianity and other living religions of the world—including modern secular religions of humanism, communism, and utopian democracy."[25]

Second, the 1972 *Discipline* affirmed protesting theologies: "black theology, female liberation theology, political and ethnic theologies, third-world theology, and theologies of human rights."[26] A few sentences later, the *Discipline* notes that these protesting theologies "agree in their demands for human dignity, true liberty, and genuine community. Since these aspirations are inherent elements in God's original design for his highest creation, we cannot resent or deny the positive objectives these theologies espouse, nor withhold support from their practical implementation."[27]

The third and, Outler thought, most important feature of the theological climate of the 1970s was "historical consciousness"[28]—each biblical book and every doctrinal statement is the product of a particular time and place, and whenever one of these is studied it is absorbed by minds shaped by a different time and place. This means that the Articles of Religion and Confession of Faith should be interpreted "appreciatively, in their historical contexts," acknowledging that "God's eternal Word never has been, nor can be, exhaustively expressed in any single form of words."[29]

This historical outlook undergirded resolutions adopted by the 1968 and 1970 General Conferences but not included in subsequent books of *Resolutions*. In 2000, the 1970 resolution was re-adopted. It acknowledges that "one of the virtues of historical insight [is] that it enables persons in a later age to recognize the circumstances of earlier events and documents."[30] The instance in mind was the sharp anti-Roman Catholic thrust of seven of the Methodist Articles of Religion. In the sixteenth century, when those Articles were drafted, Protestants were nasty in their anti-Catholic polemics, and vice versa. In the 1960s and 1970s, however, Catholics and Protestants were concentrating more on their common beliefs than on their differences. So the resolution declared the intention of United Methodists to interpret their statements of faith adopted in earlier times and circumstances "in consonance with our best ecumenical insights and judgments."[31]

This historical consciousness with regard to doctrinal statements and all the other material contained in the 1972 *Discipline*'s section on "Doctrine and Doctrinal Statements" gradually reached the desks of pastors and, more slowly, the tables of lay discussion groups. Before long, "pluralism" was a four-letter word in United Methodism.

1972–88: Is Pluralism a Nine- or Four-letter Word?

Many United Methodists accepted pluralism as a nine-letter word— acknowledgment that just as a ray of light is refracted into a spectrum of colors when it passes through a prism, so the Bible's message is refracted into a spectrum of theologies as it passes through minds polished by distinctive heritages and experiences. This positive view of pluralism led to welcoming books with titles suggesting a fiesta of theological diversity: *God Is Red: A Native View of Religion* (Vine Deloria, Jr., 1973), *Doing Theology in a Revolutionary Situation* (José Míguez Bonino, 1975), *Dark Salvation: The Story of Methodism as It Developed among Blacks in America* (Harry V. Richardson, 1976), *God, Christ, Church: A Practical Guide to Process Theology* (Marjorie Hewitt Suchocki, 1982), and *Sexism and God-Talk: Toward a Feminist Theology* (Rosemary Radford Ruether, 1983).

The United Methodist Women studied topics such as "Justice, Liberation and Development: Christian Imperatives" (1973), "Education for Global Consciousness" (1974), "Partners in Pluralism: Cultural Difference and Christian Responsibility" (1981), "Pilgrimage of Faith: Oneness in Christ" (1982), "Swords into Plowshares: Visions of Peace" (1984), "Daniel: A Tract for Troubled Times" (1985), and "Faces of Poverty in Our Midst" (1988).[32] Often it was the women of United Methodism, more than their pastors, who brought to local churches the new theologies for a new day and world that they learned at their schools of mission and at other study experiences.

Following the 1972 General Conference, pluralism for many United Methodists was a nine-letter word. They embraced permission to study, while holding to Christ, all methodologies for uncovering truth, whether those of the arts or the sciences, because, in the words of the 1972 *Discipline*, "all truth is from God."[33] Reproductions of masterpieces of Christian art from the fifth century through the twentieth found a place in church school lessons for high-school youth to help them explore dimensions of their God-given freedom beyond the customary close-in boundaries.[34]

Other United Methodists recoiled from pluralism as from a blurted out four-letter word. Pluralism represents an "abomination," Charles Keysor and Philip Hinerman told the Good News board.[35] Writing in *Good News* magazine shortly after the close of the 1972 General Conference, Keysor charged that "doctrinal pluralism" meant that "anybody was free to believe anything—with no negative limits."[36] Albert Outler termed Keysor's charge "a perverse and malicious misrepresentation," insisting that one of the "clearest and most highly self-conscious intentions" of the statement "was to indicate the *negative limits* of allowable public teaching in the United Methodist Church."[37] Evangelicals countered by insisting that it is not enough to *indicate* there are "negative limits"—identifying specific doctrines is essential.

The Good News movement, initiated by Keysor's 1966 article in the *Christian Advocate*, modeled doctrinal specificity in its 1975 Junaluska Affirmation, singling out these doctrines: the Trinity; Christ, "Mary's virgin-born Child," who died on the cross, thereby propitiating "the holy wrath of the Father" and providing "the only way of access to the Father"; and the return of Christ, a cosmic event, which "will signal the resurrection of the saved to eternal life and the lost to eternal damnation." Concerning the Bible, the Affirmation said: "The authority of Scripture derives from the fact that God, through His Spirit, inspired the authors, causing them to perceive God's truth and record it with accuracy."[38]

Analyzing the Junaluska Affirmation, United Methodist pastor Emery Percell said it did not reflect the thought of John Wesley; Dale Dunlap, a seminary professor, added that it took "a basically fundamentalist view of Scripture."[39] Over the course of the next thirty years, United Methodist conservatives released brief confessions of core doctrines. Their debating partners countered that Wesleyan Methodism had never opted for such confessional statements. While volleys of words flew off theological rackets, Good News organized a campaign to rack up General Conference votes.

The Road to Rewriting

"Pluralism was at the heart of the Good News concern," writes Riley Case, the movement's historian. "Pluralism was a legitimate concept only if it operated within well-defined boundaries, usually understood as a commonly accepted 'core of doctrine.' The Good News effort was either to delete the word 'pluralism' or to define the 'core of doctrine.'"[40] The Quadrilateral, too, was suspect. Good News feared "that 'reason' and 'experience' could be claimed in support of homosexual practice," in effect trumping "'Scripture' and 'tradition.'"[41] Therefore a drumbeat affirmation of the *primacy* of Scripture was sought.

Good News chalked up no victories at the 1976 and 1980 General Conferences. Then two things happened. The fundamentalist current that had been flowing underground in America since the 1920s came rushing to the surface during the 1970s, preparing a growing number of minds for accepting Good News's argument that "the theological confusion in the Church was epitomized by the doctrinal statement of 1972 and by the official embracing of the idea of 'pluralism.' "[42] Second, Good News drafted petitions to the 1984 General Conference aimed at specific "words, lines, sentences, and paragraphs"[43] in the 1972 statement, instead of broadly scattering its shot in the general direction of "pluralism." Even Good News found the result surprising. The 1984 General Conference passed a resolution directing the Council of Bishops to appoint a "committee on our theological task ... to prepare a new statement which will reflect the needs of the church, define the scope of our Wesleyan tradition in the context of our contemporary world, and report to the 1988 General Conference."[44]

The committee appointed by the Council of Bishops included bishops, academicians, clergy, and laity and "was representative in terms of race, gender, age, and geography."[45] Bishop Earl Hunt Jr., whom Good News identified as being sympathetic to evangelical concerns,[46] chaired the 1984–88 Committee on Our Theological Task, and Wesley scholar Richard Heitzenrater headed the writing group. Consultants from various theological perspectives addressed the committee, which decided, among other things, to omit "pluralism" from the new doctrinal statement, to reflect the global nature of United Methodism, to be inclusive in concept and language, to stress the primacy of Scripture, to endorse modern biblical criticism, and to identify Wesley's *Sermons* and *Explanatory Notes Upon the New Testament* as sources of United Methodist doctrine.[47]

When selections from the draft statement were published in the February 1987 issue of *Circuit Rider*, theological liberals, of whom John Cobb Jr. is representative, regretted the way the draft's fortissimo playing of Scripture's primacy reduced to a pianissimo accompaniment the Quadrilateral's other three elements—tradition, experience, and reason. "The issue," Cobb wrote, "is whether United Methodists should also appeal to all members of the quadrilateral as carrying authority in their own right. The statement now [1987] in the Discipline supports us in doing so. The new statement does not."[48] Cobb also found the new statement's failure to acknowledge "the authority of science" worrisome. He foresaw Creationists using the draft statement's heavy stress on the primacy of Scripture to buttress their argument that the creation narratives in Genesis present an alternative to evolution as a scientific explanation of the beginning of the world.[49]

Good News, looking at the draft from an evangelical perspective, saw it addressing "all of the Good News concerns."[50] Professor Kenneth Kinghorn, a member of the drafting committee, countered Cobb's objection to the draft's heavy emphasis on the primacy of the Bible, saying, "The Bible is the decisive source of authority."[51] A meeting of United Methodist evangelicals in Houston, Texas, in December 1987 boosted support for the draft, but complained about "abandoning the name of God, Father, Son and Holy Spirit."[52] The drafting committee had decided to delete all names and formulas, such as Father-Son-Holy Spirit and Creator-Redeemer-Sustainer, settling for affirmation of "the triune God."[53] No, argued the Houston Declaration; to do so is "to deny the revelation attested in the Scriptures."[54]

Early in 1988, another conservative objection to the draft statement found a voice in Gerald Anderson, a clergy member of the Western Pennsylvania Conference, who said that "a serious theological weakness is created" by the draft statement's failure to "suggest that *everyone needs* Jesus Christ for salvation." "If," he continued, "it is now the position of the church that God is not only present and active among people of other faiths, but that people may be saved *in and through other faiths*—without affirmation of personal faith in Jesus Christ—we need to say so for the guidance and instruction of our members."[55]

1988—Doctrinal Standards and Our Theological Task

The 1988 General Conference, by "a vote of 826 to 52,"[56] adopted, after revising it slightly, the statement prepared by the 1984–88 Committee on Our Theological Task, and incorporated it in the *Discipline* as Part II, "Doctrinal Standards and Our Theological Task."[57] It unfolds clearly, beginning with beliefs that United Methodists share with other Christians. Regarding the commonly held doctrine of the Trinity, a General Conference legislative committee, voting 41 to 39, added "Father, Son, and Holy Spirit" to the draft statement's affirmation of "the triune God."[58] Next comes a list of distinctive United Methodist beliefs, including insistence that "love of God is always linked with love of neighbor, a passion for justice and renewal in the life of the world."[59]

This is followed by an assertion quoted, with a telling change, from the 1972 doctrinal statement. In response to the outcry against *pluralism*, the 1988 statement substitutes "theological diversity" for "doctrinal pluralism,"[60] saying: "Even as [the pioneers of the United Methodist tradition] were fully committed to the principles of religious toleration and theological diversity, they were equally confident that there is a 'marrow' of Christian truth that can be identified and that must be conserved."[61] In the next section, a review of United Methodism's doctrinal history precedes enumeration of the church's sources of doctrine: the Articles of Religion, the Confession of Faith, John Wesley's *Sermons* and *Explanatory Notes Upon the New Testament,* and the General Rules.[62] Then the Quadrilateral—Scripture, tradition, experience, reason—is delineated, emphasizing Scripture's *primacy* but also acknowledging that "careful historical, literary, and textual studies ... have enriched our understanding of the Bible."[63] In conclusion, the 1988 statement calls United Methodists "to work within our diversity while exercising patience and forbearance with one another. Such patience stems neither from indifference toward truth nor from indulgent tolerance of error but from an awareness that we know only in part and that none of us is able to search the mysteries of God except the Spirit of God."[64]

The Theological Center, under Attack, Holds

What stands out in the 1988 doctrinal statement, when seen in the context of the outbreak of right-wing religion during United Methodism's first forty years, is the way the statement kept United Methodism from veering far to the theological right. In 1970, Hal Lindsey published his millions-selling apocalyptic fantasy *The Late, Great Planet Earth,* which identified the founding of the state of Israel in 1948 as the kickoff for God's end-game. By 2006, one in three Americans believed that Israel's creation was a step toward the Second Coming.[65] Fundamentalist Jerry Falwell founded the Moral Majority in 1979, launching his career of speaking, in John Wesley's phrase, "as from God"[66] on political, scientific, and moral issues. A newly confident political-religious right encouraged Pat Robertson, a tongues-speaking televangelist, to make a bid for the Republican presidential candidacy in 1988.

Viewed against the background of right-wing religion's increasing saturation of American culture, the position of The United Methodist Church is middle of the road. While affirming that "we participate in the first fruits of God's coming reign and pray in hope for its full realization on earth as in heaven,"[67] the 1988 doctrinal statement encourages "the careful historical, literary, and textual studies"[68] of the Bible that invalidate the Armageddon theories put forward in *The Late, Great Planet Earth.* Although Wesley on one occasion pooh-poohed an end-of-the-world prediction and on another himself suggested 1836 as the time when

Satan would be imprisoned, mainstream Methodism has refused to speculate on the world's sell-by date.[69] Armageddon religion—despite the way its view of an apocalyptic battle between Good and Evil seeped into American political rhetoric—never penetrated United Methodism's theological core. Two other questions, however, kept the theological middle ground unstable: "Is Jesus the only way?" and "Does the Bible contain dross as well as gold?"

Is Jesus the Only Way?

United Methodist evangelicals detected too much wiggle room in the 1988 doctrinal statement's words about witnessing to Jesus Christ: "A convincing witness to our Lord and Savior Jesus Christ...cannot fully describe or encompass the mystery of God."[70] Does this hold open the possibility that in the mystery of God's grace there is salvation outside commitment to Jesus Christ? Worrying about such openness, along with "issues around homosexuality,"[71] a group of "moderate and evangelical church leaders"[72] gathered in Memphis, Tennessee, in January 1992, and affirmed that Jesus Christ "is God's only way of salvation."[73] Dealing with this type of categorical affirmation, Wesley scholar Theodore Runyon called attention to an Article of Religion of the Church of England that Wesley *omitted* when, in 1784, he selected Articles for American Methodists—the Article declaring that eternal salvation is obtainable "only by the name of Christ."[74] Then Runyon summarized a number of Wesley quotations as laying down that "everyone who is open to the Spirit, to God's inward voice, can come to a rudimentary saving relationship to God."[75]

In 1754, Wesley, commenting on Acts 10:35, argued that persons of all nations who revere God as great, good, and wise; who stand in awe of God as the initiator and concluder of all things; and who avoid all known evils and do all the good they can, are accepted by God, through Christ, even though they do not know Christ; this "assertion," Wesley underscored, "is express, and admits of no exception."[76] Thirty years later, he asserted: "This we know, that he is not the God of the Christians only, but the God of the heathens also; that he is 'rich in mercy to all that call upon him,' 'according to the light they have'; and that 'in every nation he that feareth God and worketh righteousness is accepted of him.'"[77] Wesley's nuanced view did not echo, however, in the affirmations issued by the Confessing Movement, which was launched by United Methodist conservatives in 1994. The 1995 Confessing Statement asserted that Jesus "is the one and only Savior of the world."[78]

As their church neared age forty, United Methodists continued to give different answers to the question, *Is Jesus the only way?*

Does the Bible Contain Dross as Well as Gold?

Seminary professor Philip Wogaman attempted at the 1988 General Conference to amend the 1988 doctrinal statement's section on Scripture by inserting: "We recognize that Scripture contains both authoritative witness to the Word of God and expressions of human and cultural limitation." The closeness of the vote that rejected Wogaman's motion (454 yes, 498 no)[79] highlights the debate within United Methodism about which passages of Scripture are by-products of history and which contain eternal truths of God.

Homosexuality supplied the field on which liberals and conservatives struggled with the question of biblical authority, just as slavery provided the battlefield for a similar contest during the first half of the nineteenth century. Both sides admitted the presence of *some* "expressions of human and cultural limitation" in the Bible. The conservative Indianapolis Affirmation (1999) celebrated United Methodism's "commitment to racial and gender inclusiveness,"[80] thereby agreeing, implicitly, that certain passages of Scripture—for example, those used to defend slavery, segregation, and the subjection of women—were products of a particular time and place. But the scriptural condemnations of same-sex practices, insisted Good News and the Confessing Movement, were not such products.

The key question, as phrased by Harvard moral theologian Peter Gomes, is: "When the Bible speaks of homosexuality, does it mean what we mean when we speak of homosexuality?"[81] Liberals answer no, arguing that "the biblical writers never contemplated a form of homosexuality in which loving, monogamous, and faithful persons sought to live out the implications of the gospel with as much fidelity to it as any heterosexual believer. All they knew of homosexuality was prostitution, pederasty, lasciviousness, and exploitation."[82] And so, in the name of God, they condemned it. Conservatives, on the other hand, insist that the Bible's denunciation of gay men and lesbians is an eternal truth of God. According to the Houston Declaration (1987): "The Church, on the authority of the Scriptures, has never viewed homosexuality as a part of God's diverse, good creation, but has always considered homosexual practices as a sin and a manifestation of the brokenness of God's fallen creation."[83]

The contest over the Bible's authority in formulating a theological understanding of homosexuality came down to a competition for General Conference votes. As early as 1974, the Good News board realized "that the issue of homosexuality would be a point of controversy" in the years ahead.[84] This led Good News to oppose even a study of homosexuality.[85] In 1988, however, General Conference, by a vote of 626 to 315, established a study committee.[86]

The report to the 1992 General Conference of the Committee to Study Homosexuality included specific things that the church *cannot* teach: "The church cannot teach that all biblical references and allusions to sexual practices are binding today *just* because they are in the Bible. Specific references and allusions must be examined in light of the basic biblical witness and their respective socio-cultural contexts."[87] Conservatives, who maintained that the Bible's condemnation of same-sex practices were not "expressions of human and cultural limitation," prevented adoption of the report, while allowing it to be distributed to church members for study and discussion.

A Center with Pullable Borders

United Methodism nearing age forty continued to be theologically centrist, although evangelicals pulled the church away from its 1972 vigorous avowal of theological pluralism. The same tugs produced the affirmation, in 1988, of the primacy of Scripture. And evangelical lobbying led to an increasingly right-leaning position on homosexuality. But the doctrinal statement of 1988—with its commitment to Scripture, tradition, experience, reason—kept United Methodism from acceding to calls for a confessional statement of core doctrines, from turning away from Wesley's openness on the question of salvation, and from outright denial of the historical and cultural conditioning of passages of Scripture.

United Methodism—Approaching Age Forty

The 1988 doctrinal statement starred John Wesley's *Sermons* and *Explanatory Notes Upon the New Testament* as sources of United Methodist doctrine. Beginning in the 1980s, a succession of publishing projects and new books helped United Methodists fathom these sources. In 1984, the denomination's publishing house took over a multivolume Wesley Works project from Oxford University Press. Four years later, it launched Kingswood Books, a series of scholarly paperbacks in all areas of Wesleyan and Methodist studies. The Wesley Heritage Foundation completed a fourteen-volume set of Wesley's writings in Spanish in 1998—*Obras de Wesley*. Three scholars from the Korean Wesley Society translated Wesley's sermons into Korean; these were published in seven volumes in 2006 by the Korean Christian Literature Society.[88] The same year, Vilém Schneeberger began working on a Czech translation of Wesley's *Explanatory Notes Upon the New Testament*.[89] Also in 2006, United Methodism's presses began running *The New Interpreter's Bible*, featuring articles by scholars from forty countries and diverse theological commitments.

One study after another guided readers of Wesley's works: *Reasonable Enthusiast: John Wesley and the Rise of Methodism* (Henry Rack, 1989); *Good News to the Poor: John Wesley's Evangelical Economics* (Ted Jennings Jr., 1990); *Wesley and the People Called Methodists* (Richard Heitzenrater, 1995); *Grace and Responsibility: A Wesleyan Theology for Today* (John Cobb Jr., 1995); *The Scripture Way of Salvation: The Heart of John Wesley's Theology* (Kenneth Collins, 1997); *The New Creation: John Wesley's Theology Today* (Theodore Runyon, 1998); *Living Grace: An Outline of United Methodist Theology* (Walter Klaiber and Manfred Marquardt, 2001); and *Wesley for Armchair Theologians* (William Abraham, 2005).

Abraham pictures "Wesley's theology [as] an intellectual oasis lodged within the traditional faith of the church enshrined in the creeds."[90] Runyon applies Wesley's theology "to issues that are of significant importance today": human rights, problems of poverty and economic rights, rights of women, the environment, ecumenism, and religious pluralism.[91] Cobb writes: "A Wesleyan theology for today...will [unlike Wesley himself] recognize that the Bible is a source of some of what is wrong with us, and it will bring critical reflection to bear upon it."[92] Collins thinks "the most problematic readings of Wesley have emerged from an unwillingness ...to see this eighteenth-century man on his own terms and with his own vocabulary." "I believe," Collins continues, "that Wesley presented on his own terms...will emerge as far more relevant to our age...than I—or any others—might have preferred to make him out to be."[93]

To train lay theologians, the United Methodist Publishing House launched *Christian Believer: Knowing God with Heart and Mind* in the fall of 1999. Thirty weeks of readings from the Bible and theologians focus the thinking of participants in small-group weekly sessions on "the Classical doctrines of the Christian faith."[94] The United Methodist Women, as part of their signal role in fostering grassroots theological reflection, continued to provide theological study books such as "The World of Islam" (1989), "Ecclesiastes: The Meaning of Your Life" (1995), "Bible: Authority and Interpretation" (1999), "Exodus: An African-American Methodist Journey" (2003), and "Children of the Bible" (2005).[95]

The Priority of God's Grace in Baptism and the Lord's Supper

Beginning in the late 1980s, United Methodists gave thought to their sacramental theology, discussing whether God is present and active in Baptism and the Lord's Supper even if the recipient *cannot* (in the case of infant baptism) or *does not* (adult baptism and communion) respond in faith. In 1987, speaking of the Lord's Supper, but using logic applicable to Baptism, Richard Devor asserted: "Without faith, it is meaningless."[96] No, countered Michael O'Donnell, "God is doing something with us and for us" in the Lord's Supper, whether or not we respond to the grace offered.[97] The 1988 General Conference acknowledged this debate about sacramental theology and established a committee to study Baptism; twelve years later, the 2000 Conference created a committee to examine the Lord's Supper. The 1996 Conference adopted the Baptism study, "By Water and the Spirit"[98]; the 2004 Conference approved the Lord's Supper document, "This Holy Mystery."[99]

These statements pivot on the Wesleyan doctrine of the priority of God's grace. God's grace *comes before* any human response to God, making a response possible, without, however, overriding human freedom to ignore, question, or dismiss God. "By grace," writes David Lowes Watson, "we are given freedom to accept God's grace, but also the freedom to resist."[100] This interaction between God's *grace* and human *faith* is upheld in "By Water and the Spirit" and "This Holy Mystery." Women and men are free to accept or reject God's power given in the sacraments, but the presence of divine power does not depend upon the presence of human faith. "This Holy Mystery" declares: "Holy Baptism and Holy Communion have been chosen and designated by God as special means through which grace comes to us."[101] God comes to us in the sacraments, whether or not we go to God in response.

The Coercive Power of Male Nouns and Pronouns

The first Methodist Article of Religion insists that God is "without body or parts"[102]—God transcends sexuality. Nevertheless the pervasive use of male nouns and pronouns for God drills into the minds of boys and girls the idea that God is a super *He*. "When Homer Simpson opted out of church once," notes the author of a piece in *The Economist*, "staying home to watch football and eat waffle-batter, he dreamed that God peeled off the roof of his house and appeared, furious, in the TV room. According to a new survey, 31 percent of Americans see God that way. He (always he) is wrathful and ever-watchful."[103] Because of the injection of a sometimes angry *He*-God into so many children and adults, United Methodists, beginning in the 1970s, critiqued the coercive power of male-specific God-language, as well as the way that using *man* to designate all human beings privileges males and suppresses females. The 1980 General Conference directed the General Council on Ministries to establish a Task Force on Language Guidelines. Its report became generally available in 1985 in a study booklet titled *Words That Hurt, Words That Heal: Language about God and People*.[104]

Although grousing about officious policing of language continued, that booklet settled for United Methodism in general the question about using inclusive language when speaking about human beings. Conservatives signaled their agreement: "We affirm equality and inclusive language in all human relationships," said the Houston Declaration in 1987.[105] The inclusive God-language debate, however, was another matter, pitting feminist and many other theologians against traditionalists. In 1987, Jay Anderson, a clergy member of the Kansas West Conference, framed the debate in this way: "Are the words and concepts of Scripture culturally determined, and therefore can they be changed in a different culture, or are they revelation from God that is truth for all time?"[106] Conservatives answered: "God named himself. To change his name is to violate God and Scripture."[107]

Equally adamant were the United Methodist women and men who argued that God is too mysterious to be fully expressed in any words and metaphors, including biblical ones; so to cling exclusively to male images of the Transcendent is to clutch an idol—an idol used across the centuries to keep women subservient to men. "As long as God is male," Marge Engelman wrote in *Circuit Rider*, "the male is god."[108] United Methodist theologian Rebecca Chopp, author of *The Power to Speak: Feminism, Language, God* (1989), asserted that "feminist theology is no longer for women only and a few interested men, but intrinsic to Christianity and Christian witness in the world."[109]

Every Kind of Theology Still Alive

United Methodism harbored divergent theologies in 2006 just as it had in 1968. A broad sampling of this variety is found in the 1989 *United Methodist Hymnal*. Its section heads reflect traditional Christian doctrines: Glory of the Triune God, Grace of Jesus Christ, Power of the Holy Spirit, Community of Faith, and New Heaven and Earth. Under those headings are such Wesleyan doctrines as Prevenient Grace, Justifying Grace, and Sanctifying and Perfecting Grace. The hymns themselves represent a cornucopia of theologies spanning time, place, language, and ethnicity. There are texts by Greek- and Latin-speaking early Christians, pre- and post-Reformation Roman Catholics, Protestants of many denominations, eighteenth-century evangelicals such as Charles Wesley, nineteenth-century camp meeting and Sunday-school song leaders, and twentieth-century lyricists ranging across the theological spectrum from conservative to liberal. Also there are hymns from the African American, Asian American, Hispanic, and Native American heritages.[110]

During United Methodism's theological controversies, the Good News movement remained true to its litmus-test doctrines: inspiration of Scripture, virgin birth of Christ, substitutionary atonement of Christ, physical resurrection of Christ, and return of Christ.[111] Bishop Joseph Sprague challenged the Good News explication of each of those doctrines in his book *Affirmations of a Dissenter* (2002), telling a seminary audience that his book was an attempt "to prod progressives to consciousness, to reclaim lost space in a constricted, theologically myopic Church."[112] Thomas Lambrecht, vice-chair of the Good News board, and twenty-seven others filed a complaint against Sprague, charging him with teaching doctrines at variance with established United Methodist doctrines. An investigating committee found no merit in the charges, observing that "Bishop Sprague knows Jesus Christ as Lord and Savior, has faith in Christ's saving and transforming power and is obedient to Christ's teaching."[113]

During his seminary lecture, Sprague called the *Left Behind* novels of Tim LaHaye and Jerry Jenkins "false," identifying them as "manifestations of the misappropriation of God's revelations."[114] The *Left Behind* books, which by 2006 had sold more than sixty million copies,[115] found readers, presumably, among United Methodist laypersons, while their clergy lined up on both sides of last-days speculation. Margaret Stratton, a pastor in Waco, Texas, said, during the Hezbollah-Israeli missile exchanges of summer 2006, that "the nation of Israel is where all the focus of the world is to be in the end times. What is happening to Israel is how we measure where we are on God's time table."[116] That is an erroneous reading of apocalyptic literature, argued another United Methodist in Waco, Robert Flowers, head of the Wesley Foundation at Baylor University. He insisted that biblical prophecy must not be used to interpret, and often encourage, the bloody conflict between Palestinians and the state of Israel.[117]

Always in United Methodism, Professor Outler noted, somebody is "urging every kind of theology still alive and not a few that are dead."[118] At the heart of this Joseph's coat of theological colors is the question of how individual biblical texts are used to ground particular theological positions. Jesus is quoted as challenging persons to be born again (John 3:3) and pressing the point that "all who take the sword will perish by the sword" (Matthew 26:52). Each is a one-off saying, yet the former has millions of advocates, while pacifists are rare. "How can neo-literalists," Bishop Sprague wondered, "interpret certain portions of the Bible literally, as they do, while they either disregard or explain away other texts of equal or greater magnitude?"[119] Neoliberals, of course, do the same thing. And the answer, for two thousand years, is that texts are taken seriously for Christian doctrine when they gain popular acclaim (as in "born again") or garner majority votes in Christian conferences.

2006—Thinking Together in Love

One of the early decisions made by The United Methodist Church dealt, as we have seen, with barbed references in the Methodist Articles of Religion to Roman Catholic doctrines. This decision recognized the time-bound nature of the accusation that a certain Catholic doctrine was a "fond thing, vainly invented"; another, the source of "many superstitions"; and another, a "blasphemous fable and dangerous deceit."[120] Although United Methodists in 1968 might have continued to disagree with the doctrines in question, such as purgatory and transubstantiation, they acknowledged that the sixteenth-century language in their Articles offended their fellow Christians in the Roman Catholic communion. Therefore they declared themselves ready to interpret the offensive Articles in the light of twentieth-century ecumenical insights, among which was deeper probing by Roman Catholic theologians into the doctrines of their church.[121] This action was consistent with John Wesley's words in his 1749 *Letter to a Roman Catholic*: "Then, if we cannot yet think alike in all things, at least we may love alike."[122]

This openness to thinking together in love led to United Methodist dialogue with Roman Catholic doctrinal scholars and theologians of various Protestant denominations. A dramatic moment in this dialogue occurred in Seoul, Korea, on Sunday, July 23, 2006, when the World Methodist Council, of which The United Methodist Church is an integral part, declared its acceptance of the agreement on the doctrine of justification signed by the Lutheran World Federation and the Roman Catholic Church in 1999. Key to that agreement is this paragraph:

> In faith we together hold the conviction that justification is the work of the triune God. The Father sent his Son into the world to save sinners. The foundation and presupposition of justification is the incarnation, death, and resurrection of Christ. Justification thus means that Christ himself is our righteousness, in which we share through the Holy Spirit in accord with the will of the Father. Together we confess: By grace alone, in faith in Christ's saving work and not because of any merit on our part, we are accepted by God and receive the Holy Spirit, who renews our hearts while equipping and calling us to good works.

When the World Methodist Council accepted that doctrinal statement, Cardinal Walter Kasper, the Vatican's top official for promoting Christian unity, observed: "Today is one of the most significant dates in the history of our churches." Agreeing, Ishmael Noko, general secretary of the Lutheran World Federation, added: "We have overcome a theological difference which has divided Western Christianity since the time of the Reformation." The Methodists concluded their acceptance statement by saying: "It is our deep hope that in the near future we shall also be able to enter into closer relationship with Lutherans ... and with the Roman Catholic Church in accordance with this declaration of our common understanding of the doctrine of justification."[123]

In 1968, the Methodists and the Evangelical United Brethren declared that their respective doctrinal statements were "congruent if not identical in their doctrinal perspectives and not in conflict."[124] That declaration made it possible for the two churches to unite, and then, as we have noted, to adopt doctrinal and theological statements (1972 and 1988) that placed the Methodist Articles of Religion and the Evangelical United Brethren Confession of Faith in a late-twentieth-century context. Perhaps the Seoul declaration is pointing to a path for twenty-first-century doctrinal reinvigoration—one to be walked with Christian men and women of all denominations under the banner: "If we cannot yet think alike in all things, at least we may love alike."

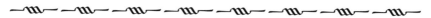

For further reading, see Thomas A. Langford, *Practical Divinity: Theology in the Wesleyan Tradition*, rev. ed. (Nashville: Abingdon Press, 1998).

CHAPTER 5

WORSHIP

After a young woman read notices of coming church events, which also were PowerPoint-projected on a large screen, the focal point of the Worship Center, she invited the casually dressed people, some clutching coffee mugs, to "begin our worship service." It started out with a soprano, accompanied by other vocalists and a band, singing Ben E. King's rhythm and blues song "Darling, Darling, Stand By Me." The lyrics cry out to a human lover, entreating the beloved not to leave, to be there to fend off fear in the dark of night. Since that song was sung to lead off worship of God, "darling" mutated into "God" on World Communion Sunday 2006 at a United Methodist church in eastern Pennsylvania.

The pastor wore, as did the musicians and ushers, tan slacks with a white T-shirt and an unbuttoned blue shirt with tails hanging out. When the time for Communion arrived, he stood at a small table jammed in between the wall and a booth decorated with athletic equipment—visual metaphors for the day's theme: "An Equipping Community." Putting aside the United Methodist liturgy for the Lord's Supper, the pastor quoted what Jesus said during his last meal with his disciples, and ushers passed baskets of bread and chalices of grape juice through the pews as a man sang at full volume: "This is my body, this is my blood."[1]

Roughly one hundred miles from that World Communion service, in a United Methodist church in northern Delaware, acolytes, choir members, and clergy, all in ecclesiastical vestments, processed solemnly down the aisle and up to the holy table, which, along with its cross and candles, serves as the focal point of the sanctuary. Children carried a processional cross and candlesticks; a woman held high a Gospel Book with an enameled metal cover and placed it on a special stand in front of the pulpit when she reached the chancel area. Above the chancel, an eighteen-thousand-piece stained-glass window depicts Jesus welcoming those "who labor and are heavy laden." The Service of Word and Table I printed in the *United Methodist Hymnal* was followed, then worshipers went to the altar rail to receive the sacramental bread and wine. Returning to their pews, men, women, and children of different races looked up at Jesus reaching out to people shouldering heavy burdens.

Neither of the worship scenes just depicted is typically United Methodist, which is the most typical thing about United Methodist worship. The traditions that came together in The United Methodist Church have a long history of official rituals, and an equally long history of laying parts if not the whole of them aside. Even though General Conference is authorized to regulate local church worship practices and exercises that authority by approving certain hymnals, orders of worship, rites for the sacraments of Baptism and the Lord's Supper, and rituals for weddings and funerals, United Methodist pastors tend to go their own ways.

Official Hymnals and Rituals

The Constitution of The United Methodist Church gives General Conference responsibility for providing and revising "the Hymnal and Ritual of the Church" and regulating "all matters relating to the form and mode of worship."[2] The first United Methodist *Discipline* declared that the hymnals of the church "are the hymnals of the Evangelical United Brethren Church [1957] and *The Methodist Hymnal* [1966]; the Ritual of the Church is that contained in the *Book of Ritual* of the Evangelical United Brethren Church, 1959, and the *Book of Worship for Church and Home* of the Methodist Church [1965]."[3]

Those hymnals and rituals were backward-looking at the very time, 1968, when the church's future, young women and men, were shrugging off everything cherished by the over-thirty crowd. The hymnals tended to be elitist, their lyrics and music vetted by academically trained hymnologists, while the rituals featured sixteenth-century *thee*'s and *thou*'s and archaic expressions such as saying that God's "*property* is always to have mercy." This was at a moment when actual worship services were often a colorful, buzzing chaos of balloons, guitars, clowns, and pop-culture English. Projects to shape new rituals were in the offing, however; they resulted in three volumes titled *Ventures in Worship* published between

1969 and 1973. A hymnal supplement, *Ventures in Song*, appeared in 1972, providing folk and contemporary songs for congregational use. But at the time of United Methodist union and for the next twenty years, the church's officially sanctioned hymnals and rituals represented the worship of bygone days—not, however, the days of the first Christians, or even John Wesley's eighteenth-century reiteration of the 1662 *Book of Common Prayer* of the Church of England, but the worship services of Methodists, Evangelicals, and United Brethren in the nineteenth century and the first half of the twentieth.

The first significant change in United Methodism's rituals came in 1984, when General Conference ended the period of trial use of the new rites for Baptism and the Lord's Supper and the new rituals for Christian Marriage and the Service of Death and Resurrection, and officially adopted them. The 1988 General Conference reduced the number of authorized hymnals to one, the *United Methodist Hymnal*,[4] which was published in 1989. The new hymnal included, placed prominently at the front of the book, a Basic Pattern of Worship,[5] detailed services of Word and Table,[6] and new rituals for the Baptismal Covenant.[7] The former Evangelical United Brethren Book of Ritual was dropped in 1992, when General Conference declared that the "ritual of the Church is contained in *Cultos Principales de la Iglesia* (1984), *The United Methodist Hymnal* (1989), and *The United Methodist Book of Worship* (1992)."[8]

The Spanish-language *Cultos Principales* was deleted in 1996, and a new book became the authorized hymnal and ritual for Spanish-speaking United Methodists—*Mil Voces Para Celebrar: Himnario Metodista* (1996). This book was not a Spanish translation of the hymns and rituals in the English-language book, but a selection of Spanish-language hymns and a ritual that, while following the denomination's Basic Pattern of Worship, was truly Hispanic in inspiration.[9] In 2000, *Come, Let Us Worship: The Korean-English United Methodist Hymnal*[10] joined the list of official hymnals and rituals.[11] No changes in the General Conference–approved list appeared in the 2004 *Discipline*.[12] But the denomination's Board of Discipleship and Publishing House issued *The Faith We Sing* in 2000, which soon gained wide acceptance as a supplement to the *Hymnal*, providing praise and worship music, new hymns, gospel songs, global and ethnic music, and Taizé chants.

The preceding narrative suggests a time of relative peace in United Methodist worship. In fact, one skirmish trailed another in the ongoing worship wars that had broken out in the 1960s.

"Onward, Christian Soldiers"

An emblematic worship-war skirmish erupted in the weeks following May 17, 1986, when the committee drafting a new United Methodist hymnal voted 11 to 10 not to include "Onward, Christian Soldiers." The next day, a newspaper's front page featured the decision as an axe job. Soon national TV networks picked up the axing, resulting in a pro-"Onward" bombardment of the revision committee's office—more than 11,000 missiles fired by July 1. The committee surrendered on July 7, and restored "Onward, Christian Soldiers" to the list of hymns approved for the proposed hymnal.[13]

This skirmish dramatizes the animosity unleashed in the worship war of United Methodism's first forty years. The pro-"Onward" camp advanced four arguments: "(1) no changes should be made in traditional hymnody; (2) hymns using military metaphors should be retained as an affirmation of the implied assumption that Christian duty carries an inherent civic duty as well; (3) militaristic metaphors within hymns should be construed in reference to spiritual warfare, which has a firm biblical base; and (4) just as other special interests were apparently being taken seriously by the committee, e.g., ethnic hymns, hymns with accepted usage from the majority ought to be considered in equal measure."[14]

The anti-"Onward" forces argued that "traditional" things are not always theologically sound. On the matter of civic duty, United Methodism's Social Principles declare that "our allegiance to God takes precedence over our allegiance to any state."[15] And yes, the Bible reports a host of battles for God and Israel, and it advocates "spiritual warfare." But just because something is in the Bible, uses such biblical metaphors as "spiritual warfare," and has a popular following, does not necessarily make it something Christians should lift up in their hymns and worship services.

The pro- and anti-"Onward" sides tell us something about the animosity mustered in the worship war, but the actual battles and the opposing forces are considerably more complex. Anti- and pro-"Onward" people were found on both sides of the major skirmishes—the one over language issues and the other over contemporary versus traditional styles of worship.

Skirmishes over Language Issues

The languages we speak emerged in particular cultures, and the concepts expressed by one language's words never find perfect equivalents in another language. In biblical terms, we live in a post-Babel world of confused tongues.[16] This confusion includes the words chosen to convey the Word of God. Nowhere do we hear God's Word in a divine language. This holds true no matter how the inspiration of Scripture is viewed; for God's Word always is couched in words born in material realities and human experiences—words whose gender distinctions and dictionary definitions have evolved through time.

Theologians understand that God is elusive; that the God who spoke to Moses, saying, "I WILL BE WHAT I WILL BE,"[17] cannot be lassoed and drawn in by words. God *transcends* every word used to address God and every combination of words used to define God. Many believers, however, assume that God is captured by forms of address and definitions; that when God is called "Father," it means that God is male-like. Identifying God with a human male troubled Church of England bishop J. A. T. Robinson, who, as we have seen, wrote a book in 1963, *Honest to God,* that jarred the God-ideas of many Americans. Robinson maintained that the words Christians use when speaking about God plant "deep down the mental image" of God "as an old man in the sky."[18] To overcome this elderly male image of God, Robinson borrowed a term from theologian Paul Tillich and named God "the Ground of Our Being."[19] Some Americans agreed with Robinson that exclusive use of masculine words causes people to think of God as a super-male, but they argued that "Ground of Being" transforms God into an impersonal force. Therefore they favored addressing God as "Father and Mother," which, as a paradox, points to a God who transcends such human categories as gender differences.[20]

At the same time that some American Christians were seeking words to make clear that God is neither male nor female, yet both motherly and fatherly, others were discussing the way the English language employs the word *man* both for males and for human beings in general. This use of *man* as a basket-word containing females as well as males has the effect, it was suggested, of making women invisible in spoken and written English. It causes little girls to grow up seeing themselves as second-class human beings, and keeps alive society's "best *man* for the job" mind-set.

United Methodists debated these language questions against the back-drop after 1980 of the inclusive-language lectionary project of the National Council of Churches of Christ, U.S.A.[21] This project's task was to provide texts for three years of Sunday Bible readings that would be free of *male*-biased words. It is "an absolute necessity for the church," one member of the task force said, "that all Christians hear their Scriptures in language that includes them all equally."[22] John 3:16 provides an example of how male-words were avoided. In the *Revised Standard Version,* it reads: "For God so loved the world that he gave his only Son"; which in the *Inclusive Language Lectionary* becomes: "For God so loved the world that God gave God's only Child."[23] The day after the *Lectionary's* publication, ninety newspapers gave it front-page coverage, and soon adrenalin gushed through traditionalist arteries. Bible-thumping critics told the task force that God is what "he revealed himself to be, and that is male."[24]

Meanwhile, the 1976 United Methodist General Conference had authorized the Worship area of the General Board of Discipleship to prepare a hymnal supplement. The task force that took up this assignment agreed to be "sensitive to the importance that United Methodists place on inclusive, nonsexist, and nondiscriminatory language." Although the eventual *Supplement to the Book of Hymns* (1982) went through several printings, it "was viewed by the church as a whole as too 'far out' ... because of its broad content and inclusive approach to language."[25]

The 1980 General Conference tried to clarify the church's position by passing a resolution, "Sexist Language and the Scripture," which called for gender-inclusive language in references to humans, but general adherence to "historic, biblical imagery" in references to God.[26] That conference also authorized a committee to sound the deep well of language from which we draw up the words we use when talking about humans and God. They discovered that many traditionally acceptable words degrade and stereotype persons and pen God in male-gender categories. These findings were submitted in a document titled "Report on Biblical and Theological Language: Words That Hurt, Words That Heal" to the 1984 General Conference, which accepted the report for continuing study.[27] The next year, a booklet titled *Words That Hurt, Words That Heal: Language about God and People*[28] was published to help local-church United Methodists reconsider the words they habitually use when speaking about God and human beings.

That study did not settle the matter, however. The next inclusive-language fray broke out when the 1984 Conference voted, by a margin of three to one, to authorize a Hymnal Revision Committee that would be funded by the church's Publishing House.[29] This decision pleased theological conservatives who thought that a hymnal prepared by the Worship section of the denomination's Board of Discipleship would be "ideologically driven," while "the publishing house was far more market driven and much likelier to present a hymnal that would sell."[30] General Conference instructed the Revision Committee "to respect the language of traditional hymns," but also to be sensitive to "inclusive and non-discriminatory language."[31]

The Revision Committee found it relatively easy to recommend Wesley, Evangelical United Brethren, Gospel, Hispanic, African American, Asian American, and Native American hymns.[32] But when they "turned to the church for opinions and help" in dealing with inclusive language, "they soon discovered a controversy with much heat and little light."[33] Tempers flared, as we have seen, when the committee tried to omit hymns with militaristic images. And attempts to lighten the heavy use of "masculine descriptions, metaphors, and addresses to God in traditional hymns" moved one correspondent to blare: "God is a MAN."[34]

Responding to this heat, the committee decided to generate the light in which they would make their decisions. They exchanged "former words of exclusivity, i.e., *men*, for commonly accepted modern words of inclusivity, i.e., *ones* or *all*." To overcome the use of "man" to signify both males and females, many familiar hymns were edited. "Pleased as man with men to dwell" became "pleased with us in flesh to dwell" in Charles Wesley's hymn "Hark! the Herald Angels Sing."[35] "God of Our Fathers" showed up as "God of the Ages,"[36] and "Good Christian Men, Rejoice" came forth as "Good Christian Friends, Rejoice."[37]

Forms for addressing God, the Revision Committee concluded, and "descriptions of God will be left for the most part as they have been transmitted to us from the richness of our evangelical and catholic hymnological repertoire."[38] In the case of new hymns, however, the committee welcomed inclusive imagery such as that found in Brian Wren's 1985 "God of Many Names," which pictures God as having a "womb."[39]

For the Psalter section of the proposed hymnal, the Revision Committee recommended a text using inclusive language for human beings and neither male nor female pronouns for God.[40] Substitutes were found for "he" and "his" in references to God in the Psalms. But when the Committee's report was acted on by the 1988 General Conference, male pronouns for God were restored.[41] Then, after the delegates added "Lord of the Dance"[42] to the list of hymns proposed by the Revision Committee, they approved all the other recommended hymns, and authorized the new hymnal by a vote of 893 to 69.[43] Almost immediately, the new *United Methodist Hymnal* gained ecumenical recognition as the most inclusive hymnal available.

While all those things were happening, there was another God-language storm. Caught in this microburst was the trinitarian formula. It was debated: Must United Methodists adhere to "Father, Son, and Holy Spirit" in their theological statements, benedictions, and baptismal liturgy? Or may they substitute "Creator, Redeemer, and Sustainer," "Holy Eternal Majesty, Holy Incarnate Word, Holy Abiding Spirit,"[44] or some other reformulation of the Trinity? The 1988 General Conference answered by declaring that United Methodists believe "in the triune God—Father, Son, and Holy Spirit."[45] That Conference also retained the traditional baptismal formula: "I baptize you in the name of the Father, and of the Son, and of the Holy Spirit."[46] And the 1988 Conference instructed bishops, when ordaining persons, to "use the historic language of the Holy Trinity: Father, Son, and Holy Spirit."[47] In some places, however, revisions of the traditional trinitarian formula were allowed. The *Book of Worship* authorized by the 1992 General Conference refers in a benediction to God, the "Creator," "Redeemer," "Sustainer," and Sanctifier."[48]

The 1988 General Conference summarized the denomination's official stance on God language in a resolution that affirmed "the right and custom of the use of biblical language and images in all [The United Methodist Church's] forms of worship and in our common life together." It did not stop there, however, but went on to insist that a "truly inclusive church will not restrict its people as to what is appropriate and what is inappropriate language and imagery about God."[49] The resolution seems to support traditionalists in their adherence to "biblical language and images" and, implicitly, to encourage liberals in their efforts to fit new God language to new cultural situations.

The first *United Methodist Book of Worship*, approved by the 1992 General Conference and published later that year, took inclusive language for humans beings for granted, and offered a wide variety of ways to avoid using masculine nouns and pronouns for God. The next year witnessed a new God-language skirmish, when more than two thousand women, including United Methodists, attended a Re-Imagining

Conference in Minneapolis, Minnesota. Central to the gathering's liturgies and discussions was "Sophia," who, according to the program, is "a figure who appears throughout the scriptures as a female personification of the wisdom of God. To her are attributed the same works of creating and ordering the universe as elsewhere are attributed to Yahweh."[50] Participants invoked Sophia as "Maker," "Mother," and "Creator God,"[51] which outraged defenders of traditional God language. Male and female leaders of the Good News movement within United Methodism argued that the conference celebrated Sophia as a "goddess," which meant the church was "dabbling in heresy and drifting towards apostasy."[52] Nine United Methodist women defended the Re-Imagining Conference, observing: "Today creative theological minds explore a whole range of issues, including the biblical meaning of God's Wisdom, Sophia (like God's Word, Logos)."[53]

Seven years later, the 2000 General Conference adopted a revised resolution on "Biblical Language." While continuing to affirm "the use of biblical language and images in worship" and United Methodism's "long-standing commitment to inclusiveness and diversity," it also encouraged the use "of diverse metaphorical images from the Bible, including masculine/feminine metaphors," the use of "language for humans that reflects both male and female," and the use of "metaphors of color, darkness, ability, and age in positive rather than exclusively negative ways."[54]

The skirmish over language issues had not ended by the time United Methodism reached its fortieth birthday. In 2008, addressing God as "Mother" still did not roll easily off United Methodist tongues, but using "man" when speaking about human beings in general revealed a mossbacked speaker.

Skirmishes over Worship Styles

The two styles of worship sketched at the beginning of this chapter stand for the opposing brigades in United Methodism's worship wars—contemporary worship at the eastern Pennsylvania church and traditional worship at the northern Delaware one. Neither side in this controversy is consistently "contemporary" or "traditional," however. Pastors of "traditional" churches may be liberal in theology, whereas pastors of "contemporary" churches often are conservative. Contemporary worship leaders may program words and tunes reminiscent of old-fashioned

Sunday-school songs; traditional worship leaders frequently select words and tunes that could only have been written in today's cultural climate. Sermons in traditional services may deal with contemporary social concerns such as economic inequality, while sermons in contemporary services may lift up traditional individual concerns such as hard work.

Significant variations of both traditional and contemporary Anglo services appear in African American, Asian American, Latino, and Native American congregations in the United States, and in central conferences in other countries. The *Discipline* authorizes the Central Conferences—Africa, Central and Southern Europe, Congo, Germany, Northern Europe, Philippines, West Africa[55]—"to prepare and translate simplified or adapted forms of such parts of the Ritual as [they] may deem necessary."[56] Churches in the United States that are predominantly African American, Asian American, Latino, and Native American have their own distinctive *ethos*, whether their worship is primarily contemporary or traditional. The 1989 *Hymnal* includes lyrics and music from those heritages, and the denomination published a number of additional resources. *Songs of Zion* (1981) provides music for African American worship, and *The Africana Worship Book* (2006) recognizes through its choices of liturgies, creeds, and chants that many persons who worship in African American churches were not born in the United States but in the Caribbean Islands, the Americas, or the continent of Africa. For Korean-speaking United Methodists, the ritual and hymns are available in the bilingual *Come, Let Us Worship: The Korean-English United Methodist Hymnal* (2000). *Hymns from the Four Winds: A Collection of Asian American Hymns* (1983) is broader in scope. Spanish-speakers have *Celebremos: Primera Parte, Colección de Coritos* (1979), containing familiar choruses; *Celebremos: Segunda Parte, Colección de Himnos, Salmos & Canticos* (1983), featuring selections from Latin America, Spain, Puerto Rico, and the United States; and the General Conference–approved *Mil Voces Para Celebrar: Himnario Metodista* (1996). For Native Americans, there is *Voices: Native American Hymns and Worship Resources* (1992). United Methodism's global dimension is recognized in *Global Praise* (three volumes, 1996–2004).

Contemporary Worship

The *Circuit Rider* magazine for United Methodist clergy featured advocates of freedom from traditional liturgical forms as 1996 flipped over into

1997. Norman Shawchuck proposed the thesis "that the worship service can be planned and conducted . . . to make it much more attractive." Mary J. Scifres identified "seekers" as the persons to be attracted, and defined them as "people of many ages and backgrounds," who "have little connection with the church," who "are on a spiritual journey," and who "are seeking a community to share in that journey." Shawchuck suggested "marketing" as "a planning discipline" to be used by congregations interested in attracting seekers. Walt Kallestad urged churches to "develop a style of engaging worship, music, and entertainment that can compete with anything on the market in terms of quality." Scifres ticked off what seekers were shopping for: churches that avoid "traditional worship elements (no altars, pulpits, traditional prayers, or traditional symbols such as the cross)"; worship that is "upbeat, fast-paced" with "practical, down-to-earth messages"; and "a creatively designed service that is stimulating visually, musically, physically, mentally, and emotionally."[57]

This market-driven approach to worship may have been new to some United Methodists at the beginning of 1997, but it was the stock-in-trade of Bill Hybels, who founded the Willow Creek Community Church in suburban Chicago, Illinois, in 1975. Outside his office Hybels posted a quote from management guru Peter Drucker: "What is our business? Who is our customer? What does the customer consider value?"[58] Hybels's research on Drucker's questions led him to remove "overtly religious images such as the cross and stained glass" and to stress "user-friendliness" and "total service excellence."[59] Thomas Long describes Willow Creek's worship style: "The services are contemporary in language and music; highly visual, employing dramatic skits and multimedia presentations; choreographed and paced to the 'high standards in the secular marketplace' of shows, plays, and other public ceremonies; filled with messages pertinent to the issues faced by people today."[60]

With varying degrees of success, United Methodist congregations across the United States took pages from Bill Hybels's marketing manual. They reshaped their worship space, or built new worship centers on the auditorium plan with a large stage around which people sit in a semicircle of individual chairs. Music stands replaced pulpits and lecterns, holy tables and crosses vanished. Sermons avoided theological discussions, centered on everyday Christian living, and steered clear of prophetic challenges to the American way of life. Praise bands with lead singers took over from organs and choirs. PowerPoint-projected song lyrics and scripture passages stood in for hymnals and Bibles. And some United

Methodist congregations grew—not, however, researchers discovered, because they were attracting people who had "little connection with the church."

Overall church attendance in the United States, including that of United Methodism, did not increase in the era of contemporary worship. Rather, reasonably large United Methodist churches offering worship of varying degrees of contemporaneity grew larger, because people shifted from smaller churches that could not afford worship excellence to larger churches that could.[61] Another study of church growth suggested that *change*, whether in the direction of contemporary worship or traditional, was the key to growing churches. Congregations "that changed their worship services moderately or more in the [five years before 2005] showed growth regardless of the direction of that change."[62]

Critique of Contemporary Worship

Critics of contemporary worship focused on its heavy dependence on the "marketing model," complaining that contemporary worship was often sold as a way to grow a church by giving people what they want, with growth being self-justifying. They also criticized contemporary worship's tendency to feature the stand-by-me gospel of Jabez instead of the take-up-your-cross gospel of Jesus. The biblical Jabez, whose name was made famous by Bruce Wilkinson in 2000,[63] prayed to God, saying: "Oh that you would bless me and enlarge my border, and that your hand might be with me, and that you would keep me from hurt and harm!"[64] Wilkinson claimed that the Jabez prayer, which is me-focused, is a prayer "that God always answers."[65] This use of God as a supernatural way for "me" to get what "I" want troubled William Willimon, at the time dean of the chapel at Duke University, and since 2004, a United Methodist bishop. "We live," Willimon wrote, "in a consumer-driven, avaricious society where everything is turned into a commodity, even the gospel, and life is said to be fulfilled only through our choices, our ability to consume cars and clothes, and even Christ." However, Willimon insisted, the gospel of Jesus "is not simply about meeting my felt needs. . . . It's amazing how many of my needs (material affluence, security, sexual fulfillment, happiness, etc.) appear not in the least to interest Jesus."[66]

Finally, critics suggested that contemporary worship focuses shortsightedly on one generation of Americans, the Baby Boomers,[67] passing traditional worship through the sieve of their cultural attitudes, with the result that many aspects of traditional worship are strained out: hymns filled with theological content; well-written, biblically sound prayers; a plan of Old and New Testament readings for each Sunday of the church year; the sermon as part of the service, not the featured attraction; and every-Sunday celebration of Holy Communion. *What will happen to contemporary worship*, critics wondered, *when the Boomers who now support it become Oldsters?* Already there is evidence that younger people favor more traditional styles of worship.

Worship Space

Before moving on to a consideration of traditional worship, something needs to be said about worship space. The relatively few churches built during the 1960s, when the Methodists and the Evangelical United Brethren were negotiating union, were modern A-frame or Colonial in architecture. Inside, both had clearly defined chancel areas with altars, pulpits and lecterns, organs, and choir seating. By the 1980s, advocates of contemporary worship were championing the "secular" look: meeting places resembling office buildings or shopping malls. Proponents of traditional worship continued to prefer buildings that "look like churches." Leaders of contemporary services favored interior space laid out like an auditorium, kept theater-dark or lighted artificially. Leaders of traditional services retained chancel and nave areas illuminated by natural light flowing in through stained glass windows and chandeliers. Traditional worship held onto elements thrown out by contemporary worship, such as the holy table, cross, candles, pulpit, lectern, organ, hymnals, and robed choirs and clergy.

Traditional Worship

Traditional worship comes in two flavors: liturgical worship based on the Order of Sunday Worship Using the Basic Pattern in the 1989 *Hymnal*[68] and sermon-centered worship based on the typical mid-twentieth-century preaching service. The latter opens with preliminaries such as hymns, prayers, one or more Bible readings, choir anthems, and announcements; uses the offering to mark the transition to the day's featured attraction—the sermon; then closes quickly with, perhaps, a call to discipleship, a hymn, and the benediction. Although the liturgies in the *Hymnal* use contemporary English, there are a few preaching-service congregations that hold onto the "thees" and "thous," the "saiths" and "begats," of sixteenth-century English.

Proponents of Word-and-Table (preaching *and* sacrament) worship focus on the centuries-old core tradition of Christian worship. In this tradition, the basic Sunday worship pattern includes reading and preaching the Word and celebrating the Eucharist. Anglican liturgical scholar Gregory Dix introduced twentieth-century Protestants to this tradition in his 1945 landmark book *The Shape of the Liturgy*. When the Church of South India shaped its liturgy in 1950, it followed the early church's pattern. Liturgical scholars in the Wesleyan tradition began training seminarians in Word-and-Table worship in the 1950s; so several decades of reflection on the basic shape of Sunday worship paved the way for the task taken up by a churchwide commission authorized in 1970 to study worship. This commission's work also flowed with a tide that rose in 1963, when the Roman Catholic Church issued its new *Constitution on the Sacred Liturgy*, which "sought to penetrate to the core and essence of Christian worship."[69]

It was clear that the typical Protestant preaching service—various preliminaries, an offering, and the featured sermon—was out of step with the glimpses of Christian worship seen in the New Testament[70] and the clear snapshots of worship taken by a number of second- and third-century church leaders. Worship in early Christian history and on up to the birth of Protestantism in the sixteenth century always involved Word *and* Table: readings from carefully selected portions of the Old and New Testament Scriptures, a homily, and sharing the "food we call Eucharist."[71] Just as early Christians believed that the Word of God became flesh in Jesus Christ, so did they believe that the Word of God became flesh every Lord's day in reading and preaching the Word *and* in the sacrament of the Table. "We have been taught," wrote Justin Martyr in the second century, "that the [bread and wine] consecrated by the word of prayer ... is the flesh and blood of [the] incarnate Jesus."[72] That "word of prayer" (now called the Great Thanksgiving) has been more or less fixed since the third-century writings of Bishop Hippolytus.[73]

With this focused picture of the core tradition of Christian worship in view, the United Methodist study commission appointed in 1970 approached its task of staking out United Methodism's place in the centuries-old tradition of Christian worship. The commission set four goals: (1) using twentieth-century English; (2) restoring the Word-*and*-Table shape of worship; (3) creating an Easter (celebratory) tone for the

Lord's Supper instead of a Good Friday (funereal) one; and (4) providing pastoral flexibility. Trial-use alternate texts were distributed during the 1970s.

The 1984 General Conference approved the resulting new liturgies for the sacraments of Baptism and the Lord's Supper, along with the church's other general services such as weddings and funerals; they were published in the 1985 *Book of Services*. The 1988 General Conference included the church's official liturgies in the new *United Methodist Hymnal* (1989);[74] also they appeared in and the new *United Methodist Book of Worship* (1992).[75]

The services for Christian Marriage and Death and Resurrection date from 1979, when study texts that included the new rites and commentaries on them were published.[76] These services were approved by the 1984 General Conference. Both are full services of worship, with hymns, prayers, scripture readings, a sermon, and the possibility of celebrating Holy Communion. The Marriage service presents the woman and man as equals, eliminates the "giving away" of the woman, and includes a response of the families and the people. The language is contemporary but not chatty, theologically strong and pastorally sensitive. This also holds true for the service of Death and Resurrection. Due attention is given to the worshipers' sense of loss, but more is given to celebrating the life of the person who died. Popular euphemisms such as "passed away" and "passed over" are shunned. Death is acknowledged as death, but death illuminated by God's love and Christ's resurrection.

The official Sunday liturgy, headed "The Basic Pattern of Worship" (which, along with the rites for the Lord's Supper and Baptism, has the place of prominence at the beginning of the *Hymnal*), adheres to the early church's worship flow: a considerable number of Scripture readings, a sermon interpreting them, and the breaking of bread and sharing of wine.[77] This pattern has four divisions, each with a number of subdivisions; and it follows the worship experience, reported in Luke 24:13-35, of the two followers of Jesus who left Jerusalem and walked to Emmaus after his resurrection.[78]

The first division, "Entrance,"[79] uses hymns and prayers to prepare persons for worship who, like the disciples on the Emmaus road, have backpacked into church the recent happenings in their world and their own lives. "Proclamation and Response" heads the second division, which mirrors Luke 24:27—"Then beginning with Moses and all the prophets, [Jesus] interpreted to [the two disciples] the things about himself in all the scriptures." To which the disciples responded by begging Jesus to stay with them.[80] Subdivisions in this part of the service include Bible readings, a sermon, and various ways for the worshipers to respond.[81]

An important development during United Methodism's first forty years was the recovery of reading significant portions of Scripture in worship. Many pastors had fallen into the habit of reading only the bit of the Bible they had chosen for their sermon, which practice stood in sharp contrast to the centuries-old plan of reading one or more psalms, a selection from another Old Testament book, and selections from an Epistle and a Gospel. The value of that plan had been recognized anew by the time that United Methodists were authorizing their new services, and the major Protestant denominations, including United Methodism, and the Roman Catholic Church, had reached general agreement on a common Lectionary. It includes three years of carefully selected Old and New Testament readings for every Sunday, following the seasons of the church year: Advent, Christmas, Epiphany, Lent, Easter, and Pentecost.[82] Using this Lectionary kept United Methodists true to Luke's statement that Jesus interpreted "the things about himself in all the scriptures" (24:27).

The third division of the Basic Pattern, "Thanksgiving,"[83] centers on what happened when Jesus and the two disciples reached the house in Emmaus: "When [Jesus] was at the table with them, he took bread, blessed and broke it, and gave it to them. Then their eyes were opened, and they recognized him."[84] Finally, "Sending Forth"[85] brings worship to a close with an outward thrust into the world that reflects Luke 24: the two disciples got up from the table "and returned to Jerusalem; and they found the eleven and their companions gathered together," and told them "what had happened on the road, and how [Jesus] had been made known to them in the breaking of the bread."[86]

The Basic Pattern for Sunday Worship heeds the advice of John Wesley, who told the American Methodists in 1784 that they were "now at full liberty simply to follow the scriptures and the primitive church."[87] By "primitive church," Wesley meant the first three or four centuries of Christian history, a period when the Lord's Supper was part of every-Sunday worship. With that fact in mind, Wesley advised ordained "elders to administer the supper of the Lord on every Lord's day."[88] The Pattern acknowledges, however, that United Methodist congregations need to be carefully prepared before they move from sermon-centered worship to Lord's Supper–centered worship; therefore omitting the Lord's Supper is an allowed option.

Worship Precedes Theologizing

When the first Christians worshiped Jesus as "Lord," they ascribed divine honors to a human being, which shivered the theological timbers of Jewish rabbis and the first Christians themselves. So early Christian thinkers set out to devise a theological understanding of the biblical Yahweh and Jesus of Nazareth that would justify and sustain their worship practice—in the words of Robert Frost: "Religion prescribed forms and for its own satisfaction found the reason why."[89] Something similar happened two millennia later in United Methodism. The services of Word and Table and the Baptismal Covenant approved by the 1984 General Conference and published in the 1989 *Hymnal* prescribed forms that embodied theological presuppositions not spelled out in authorized documents. This lack was overcome by two position papers adopted by General Conference: "By Water and the Spirit: A United Methodist Understanding of Baptism"[90] (adopted in 1996) and "This Holy Mystery: A United Methodist Understanding of the Lord's Supper"[91] (adopted in 2004); both are available in booklet form with study guides.

Many, perhaps a majority of former Methodists, Evangelicals, and United Brethren, understood Baptism as an occasion when parents vow to raise their children as Christians, and the Lord's Supper as an occasion for recalling Jesus' last meal with his disciples. The 1984-approved baptismal liturgy, however, invites God's active, *saving* presence: "Pour out your Holy Spirit to bless this gift of water and *those* who *receive* it, to wash away *their* sin and clothe *them* in righteousness throughout *their* lives."[92] By means of blessed water, God in the sacrament of Baptism incorporates the child "into God's new creation,"[93] into church membership—an incorporation that parents, sponsors, and the congregation promise to nourish and sustain until the child, maturing, may begin a conscious, life-long process of response.

Likewise the 1984-approved liturgy for the Lord's Supper proclaims that the bread and wine of Communion are *more* than something we eat and drink in remembrance of the last time Jesus ate with his disciples. "Pour out your Holy Spirit on us gathered here," the celebrant prays, "and on these gifts of bread and wine. Make them be for us the body and blood of Christ, that we may be for the world the body of Christ, redeemed by his blood."[94] In some *real* sense, the bread is "the body of Christ"; the wine, "the blood of Christ."[95] After communing, the people thank God "for this holy mystery in which you have given yourself to us."[96]

United Methodist theologians recognized that the theology underlying the new rites for Baptism and the Lord's Supper—a theology emphasizing God's activity in the sacraments—reflected the thinking of the first Christians and the majority of Christians down through the centuries. But this recognition was not shared by many, perhaps the majority of United Methodist clergy and laity, who tended to see personal faith as that which makes the sacraments valid. So the drafting of new rites was accompanied by efforts to explain their theological foundations.

United Methodism's Understanding of Baptism

A new baptismal rite was first proposed in 1976.[97] The next year, United Methodists and Lutherans initiated conversations that led in 1981 to a common statement on the scriptural meaning of baptism.[98] Meanwhile, the Commission on Faith and Order of the World Council of Churches had been shaping, as the culmination of decades of intense theological discussions, an ecumenical consensus on sacramental issues. This resulted in 1982 in a document, *Baptism, Eucharist and Ministry,* which the 1984 United Methodist General Conference urged "local churches and other units at every level of the denomination to explore" for the purpose of making use of the "theological convergence" found in it.[99] This "theological convergence" recognizes baptism as bringing "participation in Christ's death and resurrection" and "incorporation into the Body of Christ." Also it affirms baptism as "both God's gift and our human response to that gift."[100]

While the theological debate about baptism continued, the new baptismal rite was approved by the 1984 General Conference, published in the 1989 *Hymnal,* and included in the 1992 *Book of Worship.* This rite established baptism as the sole initiatory rite for the church, ruling out both infant dedication and the two-stage process of baptism and confirmation. While maintaining the importance of the baptized person's lifelong response, the rite emphasizes the primacy of God's action. In baptism, God incorporates a person in the Body of Christ, in such a way, however, that the baptized person remains free to live, no matter how haltingly, in the Body, or to live as a vestigial Body-part. Gayle C. Felton, author of *This Gift of Water: The Practice and Theology of Baptism among Methodists in America*[101] (1993), underscores this position: "Baptism is something that God does...that initiates us into the community of faith.... The grace of God offered in this sacrament of Baptism works throughout our lives as we are willing to receive and cooperate with it."[102]

This theology became official when the 1996 General Conference adopted "By Water and The Spirit: A United Methodist Understanding of Baptism."[103] It declares that "God's presence in the sacraments is real, but it must be accepted by human faith if it is to transform human lives"; and it identifies "baptism as the initiatory sacrament by which we enter into the covenant with God and are admitted as members of Christ's church."[104]

Before the ink was dry on the 1996 books of *Discipline* and *Resolutions*, the implications of declaring that baptism admits a person to church membership had tied United Methodism in a knot. It meant that baptized infants, who were too young to take membership vows, were, nevertheless, church members. This, however, contradicted the church's Constitution, which defined members as persons who had taken "the appropriate vows."[105] The 2000 General Conference began untying this knot by proposing a constitutional amendment. By 2004, the Constitution had been amended to create two membership categories: "baptized members" (persons who have been baptized) and "professing members" (persons who, in addition to being baptized, have taken "vows declaring the Christian faith").[106]

United Methodism's Understanding of the Lord's Supper

The Lord's Supper rite took on a new shape during the 1970s, with a sequence of versions printed and circulated in 1972, 1975, 1976, and 1979; the 1980 General Conference commended the latter version to local churches for trial use.[107] Two years later, the World Council of Churches published *Baptism, Eucharist and Ministry*, which reported the ecumenical consensus that the Eucharist, not the sermon, is "the central act of the church's worship."[108] This centrality was key from the beginning for the drafters of the new United Methodist rite. They continued to make minor revisions during the early 1980s, then submitted it to the 1984 General Conference for approval. It became generally available, first in the *Book of Services*, a book for worship leaders (1985); then in the *Hymnal* (1989); and finally in the *Book of Worship* (1992).

This reshaped rite for the Lord's Supper presupposes, as also was the case with the baptismal rite, a theology that many—perhaps a majority of United Methodists—found unfamiliar. They tended to view Holy

Communion, in the words of Gayle C. Felton, "as a memorial service, a remembrance of the sacrificial death of Christ." Their emphasis rested on "the human actions involved in the service," so they "gave little attention to the sacramental action of God."[109] The new rite, on the other hand, understands that the dynamic force in the sacrament is God's Spirit making our "gifts of bread and wine...be for us the body and blood of Christ."[110]

John Wesley, whose thinking was rooted in that of early Christian theologians, heralded the theology underpinning those liturgical words, referring to "the sacramental bread...as the grand channel whereby the grace of [God's] Spirit [is] conveyed to the souls of all the children of God."[111] His brother Charles declared that Communion yielded him "larger Draughts of GOD."[112] ("Draught" is the older spelling of "draft," as in draft beer.) This view confounds persons who want theology to be as clear-cut as recipes for baking bread and making wine. True theology, however, may be best expressed by poet-theologians such as Charles Wesley, who wrote: "Who shall say how bread and wine / God into us conveys!"[113] "Sure and real is the grace, / the manner be unknown."[114] In other words: *That* Christ is present in the sacrament of Holy Communion is affirmed; *how* Christ is present eludes definition. It remains a mystery. Two indispensable books for grasping the Wesleyan view of the real yet mysterious spiritual presence of God-in-Christ in the bread and wine are Charles Wesley's *Hymns on the Lord's Supper*[115] and Daniel B. Stevick's *The Altar's Fire: Charles Wesley's Hymns on the Lord's Supper, 1745— Introduction and Exposition*.[116]

What has just been said was left without substantiation throughout the 1990s. The only change in the rite itself came in 1996 when using "the pure, unfermented juice of the grape" was mandated,[117] which was out of step with the New Testament, two thousand years of Christian history, and the founders of the Methodist, Evangelical, and United Brethren traditions.[118] In 2000, General Conference authorized a study of Holy Communion. The committee's report, titled "This Holy Mystery: A United Methodist Understanding of Holy Communion,"[119] received General Conference approval in 2004. It features two sections: the first, "There Is More to the Mystery," deals with the sacrament's various names, its background in Christian and United Methodist history, and the theology undergirding the current United Methodist rite. Part Two, titled "Christ Is Here: Experiencing the Mystery," provides step-by-step guidance for interpreting and administering the rite. In 2005, the full text of

"This Holy Mystery," accompanied by a commentary and the Lord's Supper rite itself, was published as a booklet;[120] the Order of St. Luke issued a study guide for children and youth in 2006.[121]

On the ecumenical front, United Methodists entered into two provisional intercommunion agreements. In May 2005, the Council of Bishops approved an interim Eucharist-sharing plan, which the Evangelical Lutheran Church approved in August; it is anticipated that the 2008 General Conference will endorse it, thereby creating full United Methodist-Evangelical Lutheran intercommunion.[122] A Lutheran spokesperson singled out "This Holy Mystery" as being decisive in the process of reaching the agreement.[123] "Leaders from both churches said they share 'almost identical' theological understandings of the Eucharist, specifically about the 'real presence' of Jesus in the bread and wine used in the sacrament." United Methodist Bishop William B. Oden noted that "Methodists accept 'on faith' the presence of Jesus in the elements of communion but typically shy away from trying to define it."[124]

United Methodism's bishops endorsed a similar agreement with the Episcopal Church in 2005, looking forward to full approval from the 2012 General Conference. Working with the interim plan, United Methodist Bishop Bruce R. Ough and Episcopal Bishop Philip Duncan II co-celebrated the Eucharist at a meeting of United Methodism's ecumenical commission in 2006,[125] and United Methodist clergyman David G. Henritzy and Episcopal Bishop Christopher Epting acted similarly at the Episcopal Church's Chapel of Christ the Lord in New York City in 2007.[126]

Conclusion

As the United Methodist Church approached its fortieth birthday, it had an unusually inclusive set of General Conference–approved hymnals, plus supplemental hymn and song books published by the denomination; in 2007, the General Board of Discipleship and the United Methodist Publishing House agreed to ask the 2008 General Conference to authorize a study that could lead to publication of the next new hymnal, perhaps in 2013.[127] It had an official order of Sunday worship featuring a sermon and the sacrament of the Lord's Supper, which brought it into harmony with the practice of the New Testament Christian community and the majority of Christians down through the centuries. It had reshaped rites

for the sacraments of Baptism and Holy Communion, along with inter-
pretative documents, "By Water and the Spirit" and "This Holy Mystery,"
that rooted the denomination's theological understanding of the sacraments in the theology of the first Christians. And it gave pastors and
other worship leaders considerable flexibility in making use of these
materials, the products of, perhaps, the most broadly representative committees ever authorized to prepare a church's hymnals and rituals. What
was not clear was whether the denomination's bishops and district superintendents would hold pastors accountable for bringing their worship
practices into conformity with the General Conference–authorized Basic
Pattern of Worship, the rites for Baptism and Holy Communion, the services for Marriage and Death and Resurrection, and the underpinning
theology. Or would pastors go their own ways as so often was the case in
United Methodist history?

For further reading, see *Worshiping with United Methodists: A Guide for
Pastors and Church Leaders* by Hoyt L. Hickman (Nashville: Abingdon
Press, 1996) and the same author's *United Methodist Altars: A Guide for the
Congregation* (Nashville: Abingdon Press, 1996); for more advanced
study, see *American Methodist Worship* by Karen B. Westerfield Tucker
(New York: Oxford University Press, 2001).

CHAPTER 6

MINISTRY

Over the years of its life, and that of its predecessors, United Methodism has participated in God's ministry. The church "stretches out to human needs wherever love and service may convey God's love and ours. The outreach of such ministries knows no limits."[1] Ministry begins with God's ministering presence and action in human life and the compelling invitation to be partners with God through our speaking and acting as Christ's people. Ministry is both "a gift and a task." It is powered by God's unmerited grace and made visible in faithful, unsparing service to the world. Recognizing the work God gives the church to accomplish and organizing itself to fulfill God's commission are constant duties in which United Methodism has been occupied since its earliest days.

When the Methodist and Evangelical United Brethren General Conferences met in Chicago in 1966 they authorized a joint committee to study the ministry of the proposed denomination. Each brought traditions and practices that had evolved during its history. Methodists had been at work on ministry studies since 1944 and received reports from study groups at General Conferences from 1952 to 1964.[2] Studies on the ministry have continued in United Methodism to the present, the result of the church's grappling with unresolved issues. The focus of this chapter is the manner in which the denomination has sought to settle these matters over its first four decades.

Ministry of All Christians

In its report to the Uniting Conference, the joint Committee to Study the Ministry stated that although its work dealt primarily with ordained ministry, any consideration of the work of the church requires a broader view of ministry, including the general ministry of all who are baptized.

> The Committee [is] aware of the responsibility for ministry [by] all Christians. By virtue of baptism, confirmation, and responsible membership in the church both ministers and laymen share in the mission of Jesus Christ to the world. All Christians are called to ministry.[3]

While the report affirmed that all Christians are included in the ministry of the church, it carefully distinguished between ministry by the laity and the clergy. "Ministers" referred to the clergy membership of the annual conference. "Laymen" designated all laypeople, both male and female, and included lay pastors who served local churches. As the church refined its understanding of the general ministry of all Christians, these designations changed. Since both clergy and laity were understood to be in ministry, the term "minister" was superceded by terms such as "clergy" or "pastor." "Laymen," a term lacking gender inclusiveness, was replaced by "laity," "layperson," "laypeople," or the more specific terms "layman" and "laywoman."

The first United Methodist *Discipline* acknowledged that ministry is a calling conferred on all Christ's people.

> All Christians are called to ministry, and theirs is a ministry of the people of God within the community of faith and in the world. Members of The United Methodist Church receive this gift of ministry in company with all Christians and sincerely hope to continue and extend it in the world for which Christ lived, died, and lives again. The United Methodist Church believes that Baptism, confirmation, and responsible membership in the Church are visible signs of acceptance of this ministry.[4]

Recognizing that ministry is incumbent on all Christians and foundational to its mission, United Methodism added a section to its 1976 *Discipline* titled "The Ministry of All Christians," which emphasized the church's commitment to share in Christ's ministry in the world. It was the basis for the church's witness, organization, and administration.[5] Over the next six quadrenniums this section was revised and finally repositioned in the 2000 *Discipline* when it was placed after the constitution and doctrinal standards, and before the denomination's Social Principles, indicating its fundamental importance to the theology and mission of the church.[6]

Ministry of the Laity in the Church

Partnership in ministry by laity and pastors has been a desired objective of the church from its start. In this collaboration the role of laity has been, and remains, critical to the church's life. At every level of the connection laypeople have occupied a vital role. Local churches, annual conferences, and the general church have depended upon their commitment, participation, leadership, and generosity.

Laypeople have had equal voice and vote with the clergy at jurisdictional, central, and General conferences from the outset of the UMC. They did not, however, have equality of voice and vote at the annual conference because there was no provision to balance their numbers with retired clergy and clergy members not serving local churches, all of whom were eligible to speak and vote at annual conference sessions. This was remedied in 1976 when General Conference legislation authorized annual conferences to develop a means to equalize clergy and lay membership, thereby assuring equalization of lay and clergy representation.[7]

Professional lay leadership positions have been important to the church's ministry. The oldest of these is the office of deaconess, traditionally held by women serving full-time in mission work. Having a distinguished history in both predecessor denominations, deaconesses continued their ministry in the new church in 1968 and remain important. For several years their number had been declining, from 144 in 1980 to 79 in 2000.[8] By 2005, however, their ranks had increased to 124 and a correspondent office for laymen, home missioner, was established in 2004.[9]

General Conference created the office of diaconal minister, open to both women and men, in 1976. Designed to give a permanent place to professional laypeople employed by the church—such as musicians, Christian educators, and church administrators—the status of diaconal ministers was enhanced in 1992 when they were recognized as lay members of the annual conference.[10] Unlike the deaconess or home missioner who is "commissioned," the diaconal minister is a layperson who has been "consecrated." Although diaconal ministry continues in United Methodism,[11] the institution of the permanent order of deacon, discussed below, and accompanying legislation crafted by the 1996 General Conference, encouraged and enabled many diaconal ministers to become ordained deacons.[12]

It would be a serious oversight if we did not also recognize the many men and women who have served as missionaries of the church. Many of them are laypeople who serve in the United States and other nations. From the formation of the UMC they have served under the direction of the General Board of Global Ministries.[13]

Among the large corps of lay volunteers in United Methodist churches who sing in choirs, teach church school, staff food banks and clothing centers, supervise shelters, support United Methodist Women or United Methodist Men, and perform other significant service, there are a number who have given themselves to specialized ministries in the local church and community. Certified lay speakers are such a group. Methodists had an active program to train and certify lay speakers—men and women prepared to deliver sermons and lead in congregational worship when needed.[14] A similar program continued in United Methodism, although the tasks of certified lay speakers were broadened over the years to include more than public preaching and praying. They were also expected to give "support to the program emphases of the Church and . . . [to give] vital leadership to the total work of the Church."[15] In reexamining the responsibilities of lay speakers the 1992 General Conference extended their work to include caregiving ministries and instituted the position of licensed lay preacher (not to be confused with local pastor), an office with more extensive training and responsibilities than the certified lay speaker, without salary, and under the direction of the pastor-in-charge.[16] Two additional categories of lay ministry were created by the 2004 General Conference: lay missioners trained to team with a pastor-mentor in congregational development and community ministries;[17] and certified lay ministers who assist the pastor by preaching and providing support to the ministry of the local church.[18]

Many United Methodist laypeople have found fulfillment in Stephen Ministries, an ecumenical organization of caregivers founded in 1975. After extensive training Stephen Ministers offer quality Christian care to individuals in their congregations who are experiencing life crises.

Since 1812 one of the highlights of the church's General Conference has been the Episcopal Address, a state-of-the-church speech that voices the bishops' assessment of the denomination and their dreams for its future. Believing that the church also needed to hear directly from its laity, a Laity Address was instituted at the 1980 General Conference and since 1996 has been restricted to someone who serves as an annual conference lay leader.[19] Episcopal and laity addresses are published in the official records of the General Conference. A youth address, the first of its kind, is planned for the 2008 General Conference.

Local Pastors

Local preachers, the Methodist designation,[20] and *local ministers*, the Evangelical United Brethren title,[21] effectively served their denominations from the early days of both denominations. Although usually not ordained or in the itinerant ministry, these preachers were licensed and authorized by their bishop to preach and provide pastoral care to a local congregation. In order to reinforce the lay status of this category when the UMC was formed, they were designated *lay pastors*. It was clear, however, that a lay pastor was a layperson properly licensed to preach and perform the duties of a pastor except the administration of the sacraments.[22]

Major legislative changes in 1976 changed the title *lay pastor* to *local pastor* and, when properly recommended and approved by the clergy members of the annual conference, local pastors were permitted to administer the sacraments in the charge to which they were appointed.[23] This action gave local pastors a significant privilege they had not previously enjoyed. Baptizing and presiding at the Lord's Supper were prerogatives previously reserved to those who were ordained. To some, authorizing unordained local pastors, even those serving fulltime, to engage in sacramental administrations was a mistake that denigrated the unique significance of the sole right of the ordained to administer the sacraments. The 1976 legislation also granted local pastors the right to speak on the floor of the annual conference, but not to vote. By 1980, however, full-time local pastors were considered clergy members of the annual conference with voice and vote on all matters except constitutional amendments, electing delegates to General, jurisdictional, or central conferences, and matters pertaining to the ordination, character, and conference relations of clergy.[24] In 1996 part-time local pastors also gained status as clergy members of the annual conference with the same restrictions on voting privileges as their full-time local pastor counterparts.[25] Student local pastors, those enrolled in theological or pre-theological schools and serving part-time in appointments, were granted voice but no vote at annual conference by the 1980 General Conference.[26]

The number of full-time and part-time local pastors under appointment in both the United States and the central conferences has increased steadily in recent years. In 1997 the number was 4,477 in the United States, compared to 6,552 in 2004, an increase of 32 percent. Central conference local pastors numbered 2,908 in 1997 and 4,934 by 2004, an increase of 41 percent and outnumbering ordained clergy by 682 (4,934 to 4,252).

It is likely that the number of local pastors will increase in the foreseeable future and that their role in the denomination's life will become more important. As churches presently served by full-time ordained pastors find it more difficult to meet their local, annual conference, and denominational financial obligations, they will be compelled to request the appointment of full-time or part-time local pastors whose salaries and benefits are more modest than full clergy members of the annual conference. Called, committed, and well-trained local pastors have a critical role to play in the denomination's present and future ministry.

Ministry of the Ordained

Before the predecessor churches joined in 1968, each had a different tradition of ordination. Evangelical United Brethren ordained only to the order of elder. Following the precedent established by John Wesley, however, Methodists had a two-step ordination. Qualified candidates were first ordained to the order of deacon, and upon completing their theological education and fulfilling other requirements were ordained to the office of elder.

When the churches united a report from the joint Committee to Study the Ministry proposed that the Methodist practice be incorporated into the new denomination.[27] Interestingly, a ministry study conducted in 1960–64 by the Methodists recommended one ordained order, that of elder, and an unordained office of deacon.[28] The 1964 Methodist General Conference failed to adopt the report, undoubtedly believing that major changes in the matter of ministry should be postponed in light of the contemplated union with the Evangelical United Brethren.[29]

Unresolved questions about ministry, especially ministry of the ordained, led to studies in every quadrennium since the denomination's inception and reports were received by every General Conference from 1972 to 1996. Another report was commissioned in 2004.[30]

Perhaps the most significant study was presented in 1996 by the Council of Bishops in which a number of important observations and proposals were made regarding the church's ministry.[31] The Council observed that the distinction between the general ministry of all Christians and what was designated "representative ministry," a category instituted in

1980 that included both diaconal and ordained ministry, was no longer useful.[32] They noted that there was "much confusion among our people, and even among our representative ministers, about just whom a representative minister is supposed to represent."[33] To correct this confusion the bishops made two proposals.

First, a new local church office to be titled *lay ministry steward* was recommended. One or more persons, elected annually by the local charge conference, were to work with "ordained ministers to enable the local congregation to respond faithfully in ministry."[34] These laypersons were to act as congregational leaders, guides, teachers, liturgists, occasional preachers, and advocates for community justice.

Second, the term "set apart" ministry was substituted for "representative ministry" for those who are ordained. Persons called and "set apart with prayer and the laying on of hands (Acts 6:6) form the ordained ministry within the ministry of all Christians."[35]

Two orders of set apart ministry were proposed. *Deacons* were to be ordained to "a lifetime of servant leadership to both the community and the congregation, in a ministry which connects the two," after meeting stated educational requirements and training under careful probationary supervision for two years. Upon election to annual conference membership by its clergy and ordination by the bishop they would become full clergy members of the annual conference. They were to be ordained to word and service. Finding their own place of employment in a local church, they would be appointed by the bishop, but would not itinerate. Theirs would be a pastoral ministry collaborating with the pastor in charge and they would be responsible to the governing bodies of the local church. Deacons could assist with the administration of baptism and the Lord's Supper, but would not administer the sacraments. Ordination to deacon would no longer be preliminary to elder's ordination. Furthermore, the report recommended that the consecration of diaconal ministers be discontinued after those currently in candidacy completed the requirements for the office.[36] Clearly, the intention of the proposal was that the new ordained office would ultimately replace diaconal ministry.

Elders would continue to teach, guide, and serve the local congregation, including the administration of the sacraments. They are ordained to word, sacrament, service, and order. Upon completion of educational and other requirements, and upon vote of the clergy members of the annual conference, and following commissioning, they would enter a probationary period of at least three years of full-time service, after which they would be eligible for ordination as elder and eligible for clergy membership in the annual conference.[37]

Although the General Conference did not adopt the proposal for an office of lay ministry steward, believing that adequate provision for lay leadership already existed in the local church, it did approve the recommendations of a permanent order of deacon with full clergy membership in the annual conference and continued the order of elder, which was no longer the second step into sacramental ministry but the first and only step.[38]

Major changes often cause confusion in the church. Annual conference boards of ordained ministry were especially befuddled by how to deal with persons who had begun their candidacy for elder's orders before the 1996 legislation was adopted. It was generally agreed that those who began candidacy for the ordained ministry before the new legislation was adopted should be ordained as "transitional" deacons on the way to elder's orders.

During its history United Methodism has witnessed a number of significant demographic changes regarding set apart ministry. One of the most important is the number of women who have entered ministry as local pastors or ordained deacons and elders. Methodists listed 278 women under appointment in 1968.[39] By 2004 the denomination numbered more than 6,000 women in ordained ministry, both elders and deacons, approximately one-fifth of its clergy. The number of female full-time and part-time local pastors rose to more than 800.[40] In 2006 the denomination celebrated the fiftieth anniversary of full clergy rights for Methodist women, the culmination of a struggle that began in the nineteenth century.[41] The situation was different with the Evangelical United Brethren. Although women were ordained and granted full clergy rights in the Church of the United Brethren in Christ beginning in 1889, the Evangelical Church never ordained women. When the two churches joined in 1946, the clergy rights of those already ordained were recognized, but the matter of ordaining and conferring clergy rights to new women was ultimately decided by each annual conference.[42]

A second notable demographic change is the aging of the denomination's ordained elders, especially the steep decline in the number and percentage under thrity-five years of age. In 1985 there were 3,219 elders under thirty-five, while in 2005 the number dropped to 850. Young elders represented 15 percent of the total number in 1985, while in 2005 they represented less than 5 percent. Enlisting younger quality clergy is a critical factor for the vitality of the church and its work.[43]

Superintendency

Superintendency in the UMC has historically resided in the offices of bishop and district superintendent. These offices possess well-defined responsibilities for organizing and managing the spiritual and temporal life of the denomination.

American Methodists and the Evangelical United Brethren instituted the office of bishop at the time of their formation.[44] As a common feature of their structure, episcopacy was easily incorporated into United Methodism. The Plan of Union called for all active bishops in both churches and those elected at the 1968 jurisdictional and central conferences to be active bishops in the new church. Bishops' major duties included presiding at annual, jurisdictional, central, and General conferences; ordaining clergy; and appointing clergy to their places of service.

There were differences between the two predecessor bodies regarding the episcopacy. For example, whereas the EUBC General Conference quadrennially elected, installed, and assigned its bishops for four-year terms with the possibility of reelection, Methodists elected their bishops at quadrennial jurisdictional or central conferences where they were also consecrated and assigned.[45] Methodist bishops elected by jurisdictional conferences enjoyed life tenure, whereas central conferences had the power to fix the tenure of their bishops.[46]

The manner in which bishops organized their life together was another difference between the two churches. Evangelical United Brethren bishops regularly assembled as the Board of Bishops to conduct business and make decisions on matters of church law and discipline.[47] Methodists organized as a Council of Bishops to oversee the general life of the church, but without ultimately deciding church law, a power reserved to the denomination's Judicial Council.[48] When the UMC was formed, the Methodist system of a Council of Bishops and a Judicial Council was adopted. Usually meeting twice a year, the United Methodist Council of Bishops not only conducts routine business, but also has been increasingly determined to be an important voice in the church.[49] Since union it has formulated seven "initiatives" on critical issues facing both church and world. These included the "Fund for Reconciliation" (1968), to raise monies for constructive social change; "Emphasis Upon the Holy Spirit" (1975), on the Spirit's role in personal and ecclesiastical life; "In Defense of Creation" (1986), dealing with the nuclear arms crisis; "Vital Congregations—Faithful Disciples" (1988), calling attention to the importance of evangelism;[50] "Urban Ministries" (1989), emphasizing the problem of drug and alcohol abuse and addiction; "Children and Poverty" (1996); and "Hope for the Children of Africa" (1997), which sought to raise $12 million for the church in Africa to relieve the physical, social, and spiritual needs of children suffering the consequences of Africa's civil wars.[51] The council has also issued eight pastoral letters to the denomination touching on a variety of issues, including evangelism and the rural crisis in the United States.[52] Through these documents the council has endeavored to exercise episcopal leadership for the denomination. Committed to more than drafting a document on urban ministries in 1989, the council took an unprecedented action by temporarily relieving Bishop Felton E. May of his episcopal area duties in order to devote full time to work with the council's 1989 urban initiative.[53]

Concerned about the theological integrity of the denomination, the 1996 General Conference specified that bishops have the responsibility "to guard, transmit, teach, and proclaim corporately and individually, the apostolic faith" and "to teach and uphold the theological traditions of The United Methodist Church."[54]

Remarkable changes have occurred to the Council. The gender barrier was broken in 1980 when Marjorie Matthews (1916–86) became the first woman elected to the episcopacy and took her seat in the Council. By 2004 twenty-one women had been elected, including one from the central conferences, Rosemary Wenner from Germany. Sixteen women remain active episcopal leaders. In 2002 Sharon A. Brown Christopher served as the first female president of the Council of Bishops, and Sharon Zimmerman Rader was the first woman chosen for the prestigious position of secretary of the Council (1996 until her retirement in 2004).

Racial/ethnic representation on the Council has dramatically increased. Two African American bishops elected in the MC, James S. Thomas and L. Scott Allen, became active bishops in the new church. No other racial/ethnic groups in the United States were represented among the bishops at the time of union. Over the ensuing years several racial/ethnic clergy were elected. In 1968 the first African American, Roy C. Nichols, was elected to the episcopacy by the new church; in 1972 Wilbur Wong Yan Choy became the first Asian American; and in 1984

Elias G. Galvan became the first Hispanic. Leontine T. Kelly, in 1984, was the first African American woman to be elected a bishop, and in 2004 Minerva G. Carcãno was the first Hispanic American woman. Following the jurisdictional elections of 2004 there were fourteen African Americans, two Hispanics, and one Asian American among the active bishops.[55]

Central conference bishops have fully participated in the work of the Council. In 2005 there were eighteen active bishops in the central conferences.[56] As the church continues to grow in Africa and the Philippines, their episcopal representation on the Council will increase. Three central conference bishops have served as Council presidents: Ole E. Borgen (Norway), Emilio De Carvalho (Angola), and Emerito P. Nacpil (Philippines).

Another important matter concerns the composition of the Council. Although it was clear from the beginning that retired United Methodist bishops could attend meetings of the Council, but without vote, it was probably not foreseen that the number of retired bishops in the years following union would outstrip the number of active bishops. There are now almost twice as many retired as active bishops. Although the retirees bring vast experience to the deliberations of the Council, their presence is costly since the denomination pays expenses to attend the Council's biannual meetings.

Bishops are assisted in their leadership by district superintendents who function as middle managers between the annual conference and local church. The district superintendent is arguably the key liaison in the United Methodist connectional structure. Both the EUBC and the MC had superintendents. Although they functioned similarly in both churches, there were differences in the way in which the office was named and the manner in which superintendents were chosen. Methodists called them *district superintendents*. Since they had a special relationship to the bishops under whom they served, it was deemed appropriate that bishops should appoint them. It was assumed that bishops would choose those who would work best with them. The term of office was no more than six consecutive years.[57] Evangelical United Brethren called their supervisors *conference superintendents* since they were elected by majority vote of the annual conference laity and clergy to serve a term of four years with provision for reelection. Evangelical United Brethren superintendents were stationed by annual conference.[58]

As with so many structural matters, the Uniting Conference adopted the Methodist nomenclature, calling their supervisors district superintendents, and the Methodist arrangement of appointing the superintendents for six years.[59] Legislation in 1992 extended the limit of a superintendent's appointment from six to no more than eight years if there were "missional reasons" for the extension.[60]

Methodists appointed their first female district superintendent, Margaret Henrichsen of the Maine annual conference, in 1967. By 2006 there were approximately five hundred superintendents, 25 percent of whom were women.[61]

Itinerancy and Appointments

When the MC and the EUBC united, both denominations employed a system of itinerancy in which the pastors in annual conferences were appointed by bishops to their places of ministry. Evangelical United Brethren used the term "assignment to fields of labor" rather than "appointment" since their conference superintendents were elected and assigned rather than appointed by the bishop. Otherwise the two systems were essentially the same.[62] Since everyone entering full clergy membership in an annual conference agreed to go where appointed, it was considered disobedience to the order of the church for an appointee to refuse to serve where assigned by the bishop.[63] Admission to clergy membership in an annual conference guaranteed the member an appointment.[64] At the time of union it was customary for the bishop to read the full list of appointments at the close of the annual conference sessions. In more recent years it has become the practice in many annual conferences to distribute a printed list of the appointments or to announce only changes.

It has always been a challenge to match pastors with local churches in such a way that they perform effective ministry. The process by which pastoral and other appointments are made has shifted since United Methodism was formed. In 1968 it was the duty of the district superintendent to understand the mission of each district local church and to assess the needs and possibilities of each congregation. On that basis, the superintendent was directed to counsel with pastors and committees on pastor-parish relations, and then to consult with the bishop regarding appointments.[65] In 1980 the denomination adopted a more refined and formal method of appointment-making called "consultation." Two major factors in making an effective appointment were identified: the nature of a congregation, and the talents and skills of a pastor. Through consultation with local churches, district superintendents were required to determine the size, financial health, lay leadership, theology, spiritual life, and prospects for servant ministry for every congregation. They were instructed through consultation to identify each pastor's gifts and talents, depth of faith, theological stance, academic and professional experience, and family circumstances. Achieving an "effective match of [pastoral] charges and pastors" was the goal of the consultative process.[66]

A number of issues related to itinerancy have emerged during the denomination's life.[67] One of the most important is open itinerancy, pastoral appointments that reflect the racial, ethnic, and gender diversity of the church. Methodists encouraged the appointment of pastors "without regard to race or color" in 1964, undoubtedly under the influence of the civil rights movement in the United States.[68] By 1980 the denomination officially referred to its "commitment to an open itinerancy," affirming that appointments were to be made on the basis of a pastor's calling and gifts, and on the needs of congregations and institutions, regardless of the race, ethnicity, or gender of the appointee.[69] Open itinerancy was reiterated and expanded in 2004 when the church said, "Open [intinerancy] means appointments are made without regard to race, ethnic origin, gender, color, disability, marital status, or age, except for the provisions of mandatory retirement."[70] Although the denomination has made clear pronouncements about open itinerancy and many appointments fulfill this ideal, many pastors in such appointments have encountered the type of discrimination that the legislation aimed to eliminate. Denominational commitment to open itinerancy has not always translated into acceptance of women and racial/ethnic pastors by local churches.

A second issue largely pertains to the personal life and family of itinerant clergy. In making appointments bishops and district superintendents have found themselves giving greater consideration to working clergy spouses and clergy children. Decades ago, uprooting spouses from established careers and lucrative positions was not problematic since most spouses were not employed. Nor did it seem difficult to have preachers' children leave behind friends and move to new school districts. And what about the need to live closer to aging and ill parents? Appointments of married couples, both of whom are clergy, can present another challenge. If appointed to different churches, how far distant can they live and in whose parsonage will they reside? Furthermore, giving housing allowances to clergy rather than providing parsonages has often made moves more complicated. The financial complexities of buying and selling a home have proved a significant roadblock for clergy considering a new appointment.

Itinerant elders not serving local churches have encountered a third issue. At various times these clergy have been called "special appointments,"[71] "appointments beyond the local church,"[72] and "appointment to extension ministries."[73] District superintendents and ordained conference staff occupy extension appointment positions and are usually highly regarded for their ministries in an annual conference. Hospital and college chaplains, seminary professors, workers in church agencies, and others who are also appointed itinerant elders are sometimes treated as though they are not truly annual conference members because they are not serving local churches.

Tensions that have developed among ordained elders, ordained deacons, and local pastors are a fourth issue. Although elders and deacons have been considered full clergy members of the annual conference since 1996, the fact that deacons are not authorized to administer the sacraments has led some elders to believe that the ministry of deacons is not as important as theirs. Furthermore, many local pastors have expressed a deep concern that they are treated as second-class clergy by both deacons and elders. Uneasy relationships among deacons, elders, and local pastors about the roles of each in set apart ministry remains an issue with which the church wrestles.

Education and Seminaries

Methodists and the Evangelical United Brethren affirmed the importance of education for their laypeople and clergy. Each had church-related educational institutions for training their people. United Methodism inherited a significant number of secondary schools, colleges, universities, and theological seminaries when the two united.[74] Since union, a major question faced by both the church and its educational institutions, especially its colleges and universities, has been, *What does it mean to be a church-related school and a college/university-related church?* Church and schools have struggled with that issue for decades. The question took on new meaning as the church found it increasingly difficult to provide significant financial support to its schools, and many distanced themselves from the church by minimizing or even concealing their denominational relatedness.

The church's relationship to its theological seminaries has not been as problematic. An early ministry study prepared for the 1972 General Conference dealt with the importance of theological education for clergy and the denomination's support of its theological schools.[75] The report praised the establishment of the Ministerial Education Fund in 1968. During 1970, its first year, the fund distributed more than $3.5 million to the church's seminaries for operating expenses,[76] and seminaries have continued to depend upon it as a major source of their income.

There were fourteen United Methodist seminaries when the church was formed. In the name of stewardship and fiscal responsibility the 1972 ministry study voiced concern about the need for all of these schools. It recommended that the church not maintain denominational schools located too closely to one another. Special attention was paid to the four seminaries along the eastern seaboard (Boston University School of Theology, Drew University Theological School, Wesley Theological Seminary, and Duke Divinity School) and recommended the number be reduced to three. A second proposal suggested the merger of schools in the Chicago area (Garrett Theological Seminary and Evangelical Theological Seminary). A third recommendation advocated the union of two Ohio schools (Methodist Theological School in Ohio and United Theological Seminary). Six other seminaries would continue in their locations.[77] Only one of the proposals was implemented when the two Chicago area schools combined as Garrett-Evangelical Theological Seminary in 1974.

Thirteen seminaries in the United States are the official theological schools of the UMC, although many candidates for United Methodist ministry attend other accredited schools. There are also UMC or United Methodist-related seminaries located in Angola, Argentina, Austria, Brazil, Cuba, Congo, Estonia, Germany, Mozambique, Norway, Poland, Russia, Sweden, and the Philippines.[78]

Continuing education was another theme of the 1972 study. Just as most professions were emphasizing the importance of broadening and deepening one's knowledge and experience, the church recognized that its pastors and leaders must attend to their theological and spiritual development.[79] The report urged "that high priority be given to an aggressive program of initiating, correlating, promoting, and subsidizing continuing education for the ministry of The United Methodist Church."[80]

Although the denomination did not develop the "aggressive program" that the report sought, it underscored the importance of continuing education and spiritual formation for its ordained clergy and local pastors.[81]

Ministry at Forty

Ministry has been a key issue in the development of United Methodism. Both churches brought to the 1968 union an emphasis on the partnership of laity and pastors in ministry. Maintaining a healthy relationship between them has been a priority.

Questions raised over the past four decades, however, remain. How will the church deal with the aging of its supply of ordained elders? If the church becomes more dependent upon local pastors, especially part-time pastors, to lead congregations, will those appointed be adequately prepared and trained to be in charge? Will deacons, elders, and local pastors understand and honor one another as persons responding to God's call to leadership in the church? In light of the pressures on it, will itinerancy survive? Although the ministry of women and racial/ethnic persons has been officially affirmed by the denomination, will their colleagues in ministry and the congregations they serve treasure and support their work? Will the best persons—theologically, spiritually, and administratively—be appointed district superintendents or elected to the episcopacy? These and other questions beg for answers that reflect God's grace and the wisdom of the church.

For further reading, see Thomas Edward Frank, *Polity, Practice, and the Mission of The United Methodist Church* (Nashville: Abingdon Press, 2006) and John E. Harnish, *The Orders of Ministry in The United Methodist Church* (Nashville: Abingdon Press, 2000).

MISSION

W hat is the mission of the church? More specifically, what is the mission of The United Methodist Church? The answer to that question is intimately related to other chapters in this book. For United Methodism, connectionalism, theology, worship, ministry, and social engagement have a bearing on who we are, what we believe God is calling us to do in the world, and how we respond to God's summons.

Mission Statements

In the earliest days of Methodism, John Wesley and his preachers struggled with the question of the purpose and mission of the fledgling movement. They asked, "What may we reasonably believe to be God's design in raising up the Preachers called Methodist?" They answered, "Not to form any new sect; but to reform the nation, particularly the Church; and to spread scriptural holiness over the land."[1] In their first *Book of Discipline*, published in 1785, American Methodists closely followed the statement formulated by their British forebears. Their stated mission was "to reform the Continent, and to spread scriptural Holiness over these Lands."[2] Plainly, Methodists, whether in Britain or America, were not content with setting their sights too low.

Over the ensuing centuries Methodists, Evangelicals, and United Brethren endeavored to accomplish their perceived mission both in North America and abroad. Histories of their mission work tell the story of their involvement.[3] In 1999 the denomination's General Board of Global Ministries initiated the publication of a series of six volumes that provide readable accounts of mission history not previously available. Between 2003 and 2005 this series included volumes on the Evangelical United Brethren; the Methodist Protestant Church; the Methodist Episcopal Church, South; the Methodist Church; and The United Methodist Church.[4] They offer overviews and insights on the theology and development of denominational mission strategies and accomplishments.

Prior to the 1968 union, both the Evangelical United Brethren and Methodists had official mission statements that applied to their work in the United States and the larger world. The Evangelical United Brethren statement read:

> The supreme aim of missions is to make Jesus Christ known as the divine Savior of all peoples, to lead them to become Christians, to gather such disciples into Christian churches and to co-operate with these churches in building the kingdom of God and promoting world Christian fellowship.[5]

In a similar statement, although reasons for the resemblance are not known, Methodists announced their mission:

> The supreme aim of missions is to make the Lord Jesus Christ known to all peoples in all lands as their divine Savior, to persuade them to become his disciples, and to gather these disciples into Christian churches; to enlist them in the building of the kingdom of God; to co-operate with these churches; to promote world Christian fellowship; and to bring to bear on all human life the spirit and principles of Christ.[6]

When The United Methodist Church was formed, its mission statement, like those of its predecessors, was published under the disciplinary paragraphs pertaining to its Board of Missions. Defining the aim of mission, the statement speaks about bearing testimony in word and deed to God's revelation in Jesus Christ. The purpose of such witness is to bring people (the text reads "men") to new life in relationship with God and their neighbors. This new life includes worship and fellowship in Christian community as well as advocating justice and participating in ministry to the suffering.[7] The 1972 General Conference made some revisions to this mission statement and moved it to the introductory paragraphs of the

Administrative Order section of the *Discipline*, thereby practically making it the official statement to govern the ministry of the whole church.[8]

The 1984 Bicentennial of American Methodism moved the denomination to reexamine both its doctrinal stance and its understanding of mission. A commission on the mission of The United Methodist Church was formed and instructed to bring a new denominational mission statement to the 1988 General Conference. The thirty-member commission submitted a report to the General Conference titled "Grace Upon Grace: God's Mission and Ours," the title based on John 1:16, "From [Christ's] fullness we have all received, grace upon grace." It represents the most fully developed theology of mission fashioned during the denomination's forty-year history. The report did not recommend a mission program for the church, but set forth a broad mission statement based upon grace— God's unmerited, unearned, undeserved love—as a basis for evangelization and service to the world in the name of Christ. It emphasized lives changed by grace, a church formed by grace, and a world transformed by grace.[9] The General Conference legislative committee, having spent much of its time discussing a report from the theological study committee, a body also authorized by the 1984 conference, did not engage in serious deliberation of "Grace Upon Grace." Following the legislative committee's recommendation, the General Conference referred the mission report to the church for study.[10] Although it is difficult to determine how widely the document was studied, it is likely that it did not receive the attention it deserved and was not considered by succeeding conferences.

In 1996 United Methodist congregations, annual conferences, and general agencies were expected to embrace a new statement of mission. It first appeared in the local church section of the *Discipline*, "The mission of the church is to make disciples [for] Jesus Christ."[11] Based on Jesus' commissioning his disciples in Matthew 28:18, "Go therefore and make disciples of all nations," this became the connectional mission statement, but not without being questioned. In a 1997 address to the Council of Bishops, Bishop Walter Klaiber argued that while making disciples is firmly rooted in Jesus' words, he suspected that many United Methodists would interpret making disciples simply as recruiting new church members. Discipleship in the Wesleyan tradition, he warned, includes much more. It is commitment to change the world.[12]

Following its adoption as the official expression of the denomination's mission, annual conferences were advised that their purpose was "to make disciples for Jesus Christ by equipping ... local churches for ministry and providing a connection for ministry beyond the local church; all to the glory of God."[13] General agencies of the church were reminded that their work is primarily "to enable local congregations, the primary arena for mission, faithfully and fruitfully to make disciples for Jesus Christ."[14] On its fortieth birthday, making disciples for Jesus Christ remained the operative mission statement of the denomination. In order to bring focus to their ministries, local churches, annual conferences, and the agencies of the church have been encouraged to formulate and adopt mission statements that incorporate the emphasis on disciple-making.

Mission and Missions

Since their beginnings Evangelical United Brethren and Methodist congregations have not only been engaged in mission in their local communities, they have also participated in a wider denominational mission in the United States and other parts of the world.

At the time of union the Evangelical United Brethren supported "home" mission work in various places across the United States, including Kentucky, New Mexico, Florida, and Wisconsin.[15] Commissions on town and country, and urban work provided direction for denominational ministries in various American communities. Outside the United States the church maintained "world" mission work in Asia (Japan, China, Philippines), Europe (Germany, Switzerland), Africa (Sudan, Sierra Leone), and Latin America and the Caribbean (Brazil, Ecuador, Dominican Republic, Puerto Rico).[16] In its world mission program the Evangelical United Brethren Church was committed to ecumenical forms of ministry outside the United States and was concerned at the time of union that Methodist mission work was not as broadly ecumenical.[17] Mission work in the EUBC was directed by the church's Board of Missions and funded by apportionments paid by local churches, special campaigns, and the Women's Society of World Service.

Before 1968, Methodist denominational mission work inside and outside the United States was conducted on a larger scale than the EUBC. In addition to "national" missions in rural areas, towns, and cities in America, Methodists stationed hundreds of "world" missionaries in Africa, Asia, Europe, and Latin America, many of them recruited and funded by women through the Woman's Division.[18] Missionaries were supervised by the Methodist Church's Board of Missions and funded by World Service Fund apportionments paid by local churches, special offerings, and generous support by the Woman's Society of Christian Service.[19]

With union, the work of the boards of missions of the former denominations was assumed by the Board of Missions of The United Methodist Church, which in 1972 became the Board of Global Ministries.[20] Tracey K. Jones, selected to head the missions agency in 1968, early in his new position issued a sweeping statement that explored a vision for the church's mission. He stressed the significance of personal faith and its social implications, the importance of missionary activity in the public sector of life (e.g., politics, economics), the indispensability of specialized competent church leadership to face complex world issues, participation in mission with other denominations, and the increasing necessity of all Christians to be involved in God's work in the world.[21] Jones's insights provided a context in which to understand United Methodism's missional direction during its earliest years.

During the twentieth century, while the church in the United States provided much of the financial support and missionary personnel for its work in other lands, mission work outside the United States was increasingly placed in the hands of indigenous leadership.[22] The indigenous approach continued in United Methodism, vigorously supported by such voices as African United Methodist bishop Abel Muzorewa who criticized the paternalism that characterized much of the Western approach to African missions, its inability to understand African culture, and its narrow denominationalism.[23]

Successful Methodist mission work outside the United States was organized into annual conferences, then into central conferences, which remain important components of United Methodism. Central conferences originated in the Methodist Episcopal Church when its 1884 General Conference authorized the formation of central conferences to develop educational, publishing, and other connectional work committed to it by its annual conferences, as long as there was no violation of the *Book of Discipline* or the rules of the General Conference.[24] Powers of the central conferences were enlarged in 1928 to permit them to elect their own bishops.[25] When The United Methodist Church was formed the central conference structure of Methodism was adopted.[26] Central conferences are located in Africa (three, serving more than twenty countries), Europe (three, serving twenty-six countries), and the Philippines.[27]

One of the most stunning developments in the European central conferences was the emergence of United Methodism in Russia. Although Methodist mission work in Russia began as early as 1889, it never flourished there and was practically extinct under the Soviet regime.[28] Officials of the General Board of Global Ministries visited Moscow early in 1991 to explore the possibilities of a United Methodist presence in Russia in cooperation with the Russian Orthodox Church. Within the year the Soviet Union was dissolved. The 1992 General Conference established a new episcopal area for Russia with headquarters in Moscow. After his election to the episcopacy by the Northern Europe Central Conference in 1992, Rüdiger Minor, a German church leader, was named to head the ministry in Russia. Among other duties, Minor had to negotiate with the Russian Orthodox Church over its growing suspicions of various independent Protestant churches expanding their ministries in Russia after the collapse of the Soviet Union. Proving an earlier Methodist denominational presence in the country was a key factor in Russian acceptance of the role of United Methodism and its official registration in the Russian Federation.[29] In 2000 United Methodism in the Russian Federation became an annual conference with eighty-seven congregations, sixty-four pastors (half of them women), and approximately five thousand members.[30] The church also opened a theological seminary in Moscow, which graduated its first class in 1997.[31] United Methodism also extended mission work to Kazakhstan, Latvia, Lithuania, and Estonia in the 1990s. A major accomplishment was the completion of the beautiful and functional Baltic Mission Center in Tallinn, Estonia, in 2000.[32]

Denominational mission work in both the United States and other nations has proceeded on a number of fronts including "missional priorities" and "special programs" adopted by the General Conference. Missional priority, a concept created in 1980, is "a response to a critical need in God's world which calls for The United Methodist Church's massive and sustained effort" through the program and budget of the church as determined by the General Conference.[33] Missional priorities have included world hunger (1976) and strengthening and developing ethnic minority local churches (1976–88).[34] Special programs are quadrennial emphases initiated by the denomination's four program boards (Church and Society, Discipleship, Global Ministries, Higher Education and Ministry), approved by the General Conference and specifically assigned to one of the program agencies.[35] They have included Africa church growth and development, a national plan for urban ministry ("Holy

Boldness"), substance abuse and related violence, and the establishment of shalom zones begun in Los Angeles and other cities after the abuse of Rodney King by police in 1992.[36] The shalom zone program was designed to assist churches in working with their communities "to stimulate economic development, improve race and class relationships, address health issues, and develop congregations" to produce positive social change.[37]

Recognizing responsibility for the wider mission of the church, the Council of Bishops assumed a role in forming mission initiatives for the denomination. Among those initiatives have been "Children and Poverty" (1996), which called attention to the desperate worldwide plight of children caught in the web of poverty, and "Hope for the Children of Africa: Relief, Reconciliation and Rebuilding" (1997), which focused attention on the physical, psychological, and spiritual circumstances of African children suffering the devastation of civil wars.[38]

Mission, of course, is carried on by people, clergy and laity, called by God to proclaim the good news of grace in word and act; to invite men, women, young people, and children to become Christ's disciples; and to serve in Christ's name wherever there is need. Much of the mission involvement of people, especially in local churches and communities, goes unrecorded except in the sight of God. United Methodism, however, keeps records on its officially commissioned missionaries, who are financially supported by denominational funds and who serve under the supervision of the General Board of Global Ministries. In 1970 there were 1,637, by 1980 the number declined to 1,073. Twenty years later it was 946, and by 2005 there were 497. If the total number of commissioned and other mission personnel supported by the General Board of Global Ministries is included, in 2005 the number was 893 who served in sixty-two countries.[39]

By the 1970s there was a thriving corps of volunteers from local churches, districts, annual conferences, and other United Methodist groups engaged in a variety of mission projects in the United States and elsewhere. Seeing the need for supervision of this growing movement, in 1976 the General Board of Global Ministries began to organize short-term volunteers-in-mission.[40] Four years later the General Conference placed the volunteer program under the direction of Global Ministries,[41] and in 1996 incorporated mission volunteers as a discrete program area of the board.[42] According to 1998 statistics, more than 54,000 United Methodists participated in volunteer projects contributing more than 16 million hours of service.[43] There is little doubt that these numbers have grown significantly during more recent years and that many more United

Methodists, whose participation is not counted, have contributed volunteer service.

News and information about United Methodist mission efforts has been transmitted in a variety of forms. Information about local churches, districts, and annual conferences has been communicated in bulletins, newsletters, and newspapers, and increasingly through websites and e-mails.

Important reports about denominational mission work have been disseminated through publications. *New World Outlook,* a periodical of the General Board of Global Ministries that replaced Methodism's *World Outlook* in 1970, has carried articles to inform United Methodists about the breadth of the church's involvement in mission in the United States and other countries. *Reponse,* a magazine principally for United Methodist Women, began in 1969 as the successor to the Evangelical United Brethren women's *The World Evangel* and Methodism's *Methodist Woman.* These publications have included information about the means by which local church people can participate in mission through prayer, financial contribution, and volunteering with others in specific mission tasks.

Annual mission studies have been one of the most effective means of mission education. As early as 1911 a committee of the National Council of Churches annually selected two mission course themes, "one related to home missions and one to foreign," for study by its member denominations.[44] Textbooks, supplementary guides, and audiovisual materials were produced for each theme. United Methodism, primarily through the Woman's Division, adopted three mission studies to be offered to the church annually and produced resource materials for each. They dealt with (1) spiritual growth, (2) social engagement (see chapter 7), and (3) a geographical area. Annual conference schools of Christian mission have employed these themes and have promoted their use in local churches, chiefly through United Methodist Women. Since 1968 geographical studies have included a host of nations and world areas, including Africa, Asia, Latin America, Europe, the Caribbean, and the Middle East—all designed to raise the global mission consciousness of United Methodists.

Holistic Mission

From its earliest days the church has believed that God commissioned it for holistic mission—to address and provide for the spiritual, physical, and intellectual needs of people. Just as Jesus preached the good news of God's love, healed the sick, fed the hungry, associated with outcasts, and taught the way of righteous living, his disciples of every age are summoned to follow him in holistic ministry.

John Wesley urged Methodists to engage in a ministry that reached the needs of people whatever their circumstances and necessities. In 1743, while Methodism was a young movement, Wesley wrote General Rules for his people that included "doing good of every possible sort and as far as is possible to all [people]." To be more specific, he added, doing good "to their bodies ... by giving food to the hungry, by clothing the naked, by visiting or helping them that are sick, or in prison." Methodist people were also admonished to minister to peoples' spiritual needs, to do good "to their souls, by instructing, *reproving,* [and] exhorting all" (italics his).[45] Wesley's admonition is an expression of his commitment to holistic mission, though, of course, he did not use the term. United Methodism and its predecessors have labored to understand and make their mission holistic. Three areas of mission are illustrative.

Evangelism and Spiritual Formation

Evangelism was central for both the Evangelical United Brethren and Methodists. The EUBC defined evangelism as "winning ... the lost to Jesus Christ as Savior and Lord" and affirmed "a definite personal experience of salvation and a progressive building of Christlike character."[46] The first responsibility of the EUB pastor was "to win as many people as possible to Jesus Christ, to build them up in Christian faith and practice, and to lead them into the fellowship and service of the church."[47] Evangelistic work was supported by a denominational Board of Evangelism and it was clearly stated that evangelistic work was the duty of every local church and its members.[48]

Methodists also considered evangelism essential to the church's mission. The aim of evangelism was to bring all people into an active relationship with God through Jesus Christ, to gather them into the fellowship of the church, and to lead them to give evidence of their discipleship in every area of life.[49] Local churches, districts, and annual conferences were required to have committees on evangelism, all of which were supported by the denomination's Board of Evangelism.

Both churches' statements on evangelism were incorporated into the *Book of Discipline* of the new church,[50] and the Methodist connectional evangelism structure was put into place.[51] When the new denominational structure was approved in 1972 evangelism was joined with worship and stewardship in a division of the General Board of Discipleship. It remains under the direction of the general board,[52] which acknowledges, "Evangelism is central to the mission of the Church."[53] One of the critical and disputed questions related to the evangelistic task is whether Christ is the only way of salvation, a question dealt with in chapter 3.

There have been attempts to underscore the importance of evangelism in the church. In 1974 the Council of Bishops issued a pastoral message on evangelism in which it spoke of evangelism as an "urgent concern" in the church and called for an intensive campaign of preaching, personal faith-sharing, visitation, and use of the media in the work of disseminating the gospel.[54] The Council developed and implemented the 1988 initiative, "Vital Congregations—Faithful Disciples," which had an evangelistic emphasis. The bishops announced, "We are sent as ambassadors for Christ—to announce the good news, to make disciples, to go where Jesus went, into the hurts and hopes of the world."[55]

Statistics reveal that the work of evangelism has been successful among United Methodists in Africa and the Philippines, where the church has grown significantly in recent years. In Europe and the United States the work of evangelism and spiritual formation also continues, bearing fruit in the ministries of many local churches and their people, although many United Methodists believe there is insufficient emphasis on evangelism.

Health and Welfare Ministries

Holistic mission has been a concern of the church from Wesley's day to the present. The church's mission has involved not only people's spiritual needs, but their physical health and welfare. John Wesley set the pace for this ministry. In addition to his evangelistic efforts he established housing for widows and orphans, set up medical dispensaries in some of his chapels, collected and distributed funds for the poor, and published a book of cures for common illnesses.

When Methodists joined with the Evangelical United Brethren, each church was involved in health and welfare ministries as an evidence of its mission. Ten homes for children and the aging were officially related to the Evangelical United Brethren.[56] Methodists operated a large number of hospitals as well as homes for children, youth, and the aging across the country, all under the direction of the denomination's Board of Hospitals and Homes.[57] Health and welfare ministries of United Methodism were placed under its Board of Missions[58] and in 1972 became the Division of Health and Welfare Ministries of the General Board of Global Ministries and remained under the direction of the general board.[59]

Two important developments in United Methodism brought its health and welfare ministries into the national spotlight. The first was the financial crisis surrounding the bankruptcy of Pacific Homes, one of the church's retirement facilities owned at the time by the Pacific Southwest annual conference. The retirement center had issued life care contracts to residents without setting aside protected reserve funds to guarantee long-term financial stability. When the Pacific Homes corporation encountered severe cash flow problems in 1977, the residents brought suit for $500 million against the annual conference and denomination. For the next twenty-two years annual conference and denominational funds were used to settle the suit, the final payments on loans made in 1999.[60]

Litigation and settlement of the Pacific Homes matter caused shock-waves across the denomination. With the large number of hospitals, retirement communities, and other health and welfare agencies related to United Methodism, the church became more aware of potential fiscal liability in an increasingly litigious society. To assist annual conferences with their relationships to health and welfare institutions within their bounds and to mitigate denominational liability, the United Methodist Association of Health and Welfare Ministries, generally known as UMA, was formed as an independent, not-for-profit corporation. The association helps both annual conferences and their institutions define the relationship between them in terms of mission, finances, and legal responsibilities.[61]

The second development concerns the unique role played by the United Methodist Committee on Relief (UMCOR) in various domestic and international disasters. Formed by the Methodist Church in 1940 as a response to the violence of World War II, the Methodist Committee on Overseas Relief was the predecessor to its United Methodist offspring. In 1972 it came under the direction of the General Board of Global Ministries. In the following decades, through generous contributions of people in local churches to the One Great Hour of Sharing,[62] the Advance for Christ and His Church,[63] and special contributions, United Methodists responded to emergencies and disasters around the world. Food, medical care and supplies, HIV/AIDS programs, and legal counsel for immigrants and asylum seekers were among the many ways in which the church reached out to people in the Caribbean, Middle East, Europe, Latin America, Africa, and the United States. Effective mission efforts by the relief committee more recently included response to the World Trade Center tragedy in 2001 ($17.5 million raised for its victims); the South Asia tsunami in December 2004 ($10 million given in five weeks); and Hurricane Katrina, the most destructive storm in United States history, in the summer of 2005 ($64.5 million contributed by mid-2006).[64]

Not only has the church provided food, clothing, housing, and medical care to relieve physical suffering, through its local churches, annual conferences, and denominational agencies it has also been an advocate for peace, justice, and human rights. Mission includes the elimination of racism, sexism, narrow nationalism, and all forms of discrimination, which choke off the possibilities for all to realize what God intends human life to be.[65]

Educational Ministry

In its commitment to holistic mission United Methodism has been dedicated to an educational program for the denomination. While its Sunday church schools have experienced significant declines in both membership and attendance, they remain a major forum for teaching children, youth, and adults. Other educational programs, such as DISCIPLE Bible study, have taken up some of the slack in the church's devotion to thoughtful Christian discipleship.

United Methodism and its antecedents have placed important emphasis on education as another dimension of mission. Beginning with John Wesley's Kingswood school, opened in England in 1748, and Cokesbury College, founded by American Methodists in 1784, Methodists, Evangelicals, and United Brethren founded scores of schools, colleges, universities, and theological seminaries, believing that effective living in the world demands outstanding educational training. More than 125 schools, colleges, universities, and theological seminaries survived to the United Methodist union and continue to be affiliated with the denomination.[66]

One of the principal issues involving the church and its educational institutions has been determining what it means to be a church-related school and a school-related church. Whereas this relationship was frequently visible in the church's providing funds for its schools (however modest), the church has found it increasingly difficult to make significant funding available to its educational institutions except for its thirteen theological semnaries. Furthermore, some schools, seeking to reach a more diverse pool of applicants, have become more reluctant to advertise themselves as church-related and virtually ignore the historic ties between church and academy.[67]

Among the most dramatic events in United Methodism's educational mission has been the establishment of Africa University in Zimbabwe. The dream for a church-related university originated in 1984 when two African bishops, Arthur Kulah of Liberia and Emilio J. M. De Carvalho of Angola, challenged the church to create a university for the continent. They believed that higher education was important for Africa's peace, stability, and development. Under the leadership of the General Board of Higher Education and Ministry the 1988 General Conference approved the founding of a school primarily funded by the church's congregations in the United States. Ground was broken for the school in 1991, and the following year classes began with forty students from twelve African nations. Students were admitted regardless of race, ethnicity, religion, politics, gender, nationality, or social background. From its humble origins in converted farm buildings, the university expanded its faculty and added new student residences, classroom buildings, a library, and a chapel. By 2001 enrollment reached almost 800 from twenty-two countries, and by the fall of 2006 the school registered almost 1,300 students in its five schools.[68]

Missional Controversy

Shortly after the 1968 union was consummated, controversy about missions, especially regarding the theology and work of the newly organized General Board of Global Ministries, was brewing. In February 1974 a group of seventy pastors and laypeople met to discuss what they perceived as the board's liberal theological drift. They were disturbed that the board paid little or no attention to evangelizing non-Christians and devoted too much energy to addressing social and political issues.[69] Although the Good News caucus initiated this meeting, it denied that it had predetermined the agenda for the meeting. The group formed themselves into the Evangelical Missions Council, pledging to promote the cause of missions and to initiate conversations with the general board about their concerns and what they perceived as the board's misdirections.[70]

Dialogues between the board and the council did not result in reconciling the two parties. Those who represented the council felt that the board had convinced itself that its ministry was balanced and holistic, and that it was engaged in evangelism, spiritual formation, and church growth, as well as matters of social and political change.[71] The board complained that the council's tactics were inappropriate, for example, calling for evangelistic efforts in nations and cultures shaped by other religions.[72] The conversations convinced the council that the board would not change its missions strategy. The board was persuaded that the council, in its dissatisfaction with the board, would ultimately form a new missions agency to correct what it judged to be the board's failings.

Riley B. Case asserts that the failure of the conversations between the council and the board as well as two other developments were critical to the next steps in the missions controversy. The first was the Jessup Report, a document prepared by David Jessup, a Methodist layperson and staff member of the AFL-CIO's political education committee, who alleged that some grants by the church's General Board of Global Ministries and the General Board of Church and Society funded organizations and causes with communist affiliations. His research was circulated among the delegates to the 1980 General Conference where it received no official attention. Jessup's report was attacked in the church press, and an official church reply, drafted by its communications agency, defending the agencies involved was mailed to all United Methodist clergy.[73]

A second key development was the founding of the Institute on Religion and Democracy, an ecumenical alliance formed in 1981, "working to reform [the] churches' social witness, in accord with biblical and historic Christian teachings, thereby contributing to the renewal of democratic society at home and abroad."[74] Like the Jessup Report, the research of the institute alleged that funds of various denominations, including United Methodism, were used to support left-leaning political causes that many church members found objectionable. This criticism was popularized in the article, "Do You Know Where Your Church Offerings Go?" in the December 1982 issue of *Reader's Digest* and the January 1983 CBS *60 Minutes* program segment, "The Gospel According to Whom?"[75] Despite the attempts of church leaders to characterize these organizational and media assaults as sensational and misleading, they raised questions about the denomination's missions agencies in the minds of many United Methodists.

In November 1983 thirty-four United Methodists, believing that an evangelical voice in the denomination's missions work was not adequately heeded by the General Board of Global Ministries, voted to form a new organization, not to replace support for the board, but to supplement it as a missions-sending agency. Formally organized and incorporated the following year as the Mission Society for United Methodists, and without the official blessing of the church or its bishops, it commissioned and stationed its first missionaries in 1985.[76] The rationale for the new body was articulated in an important article by Gerald H. Anderson, well-known United Methodist missions specialist and head of the ecumenical Overseas Ministry Center, titled, "Why We Need a Second Mission Agency."[77] By 2006 the Society had 208 missionaries working in thirty-one countries including Africa, Asia, the Caribbean and Latin America, Europe, the Middle East, North America, and South America.

In assessing the impact of the mission society in his history of United Methodist mission Robert J. Harman notes that church leaders in Latin America and elsewhere were critical of the Mission Society because it not only threatened the unity of The United Methodist Church in the United States, but in its global missions work.[78]

Growing out of conversations with the Mission Society, in 1987 the general board was challenged by its general secretary to create a Mission Evangelism Program Department. This proposal did not come to full realization until 1993 when S T Kimbrough brought unique theological and worship skills to bear to enrich evangelistic work and strengthen the spiritual life of the church.[79]

Ecumenical Engagement in Mission

One of the major forces in the origin of the twentieth-century ecumenical movement was the common concern that Christian churches had for mission in their native lands and in other parts of the world. Prior to their union Evangelical United Brethren and Methodists shared a commitment to work ecumenically with other churches in common mission objectives. Both were active members of the National Council of Churches of Christ in the U.S.A. and the World Council of Churches, contributing funds for their support and choosing official representatives.

As J. Steven O'Malley observes, however, there was an essential difference between the two denominations in their mission work outside the United States. Methodist "overseas" work was mostly organized in central conferences that were closely related to the church in the United States. Evangelical United Brethren mission, however, was structured in "autonomous, united churches."[80] Work in the Philippines illustrated this difference. Whereas Filipino Methodism was organized in traditional Methodist annual conferences, the Evangelical United Brethren fully supported and participated in the United Church of Christ in the Philippines, which included other denominations.[81] Whereas missions strategy of the EUBC was determined by its Board of Missions, the denomination's Commission on Church Union was authorized to consider proposals for union with other churches, to make recommendations directly to the General Conference, and to implement the conference's decisions on matters of union.[82] Ecumenical relationships in Methodism were handled by its Commission on Ecumenical Affairs.[83]

When the new church was born, the Methodist commission was incorporated into its structure. Between 1972 and 1980 ecumenical work became a division of the Board of Global Ministries, and finally was organized, and continues, as the General Commission on Christian Unity and Interreligious Concerns.[84] Its purpose is "to foster approaches to ministry and mission that more fully reflect the oneness of Christ's church in the human community."[85]

Many current Methodist denominations in other parts of the world began as missions planted by the Evangelical United Brethren and Methodists and are now autonomous churches, some of which maintain an affiliation with The United Methodist Church. Among these are the Methodist Church of Mexico, the Korean Methodist Church, and the Methodist Church of Brazil. The Methodist Church of Puerto Rico, once a United Methodist annual conference, became autonomous in 1992 and is the most recent church to organize from United Methodist mission roots.[86] United Methodism in the Philippines celebrated its centennial in 1998[87] amid talk that favored its autonomy.[88]

A Future for Missions

As long as there are people in spiritual, physical, and educational need, there is a mission for the Body of Christ, the church. Wherever people need to hear about and sense the presence and grace of God in Jesus Christ, there is a place for the church's voice and action. Wherever there is domestic violence, hunger, homelessness, war and its accompanying horrors, racism, HIV/AIDS, environmental crises, disintegrating family life, earthquakes and other natural disasters, and the countless other issues that confront us worldwide, there is need for the holistic ministries of United Methodism and the other churches that are members of Christ's Body. A statement in the 1988 proposed mission document briefly summarizes the present and future mission of the church:

> Our mission is to witness to [the] grace of God in Jesus Christ through the giving of our lives in sacrificial love: by retelling the story of God's self-giving, by inviting people to respond to God's grace, by building up the Body of Christ through inclusive love, and by offering our lives in the service of others.[89]

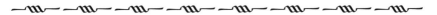

For further reading, see Robert J. Harman, *From Missions to Mission: The History of Mission of The United Methodist Church, 1968–2000* (New York: General Board of Global Ministries, The United Methodist Church, 2005), and Riley B. Case, *Evangelical and Methodist: A Popular History* (Nashville: Abingdon Press, 2004).

CHAPTER 8

SOCIAL ENGAGEMENT

United Methodism locks up its doctrine in a constitutional safe. Restrictions in the church's Constitution make it all but impossible to amend the Articles of Religion and Confession of Faith.[1] Because those documents are so difficult to revise, it is in debates about statements of social engagement that United Methodists decide if new occasions call for learning new theological lessons.[2] Nowhere is this clearer, as we shall see, than in the controversy about homosexuality.

Homosexuality hovered just below United Methodism's social engagement horizon in 1968, when the uniting conference decided to include two statements that do not mention it in the new church's first *Book of Discipline*—the Methodist Social Creed and the Basic Beliefs Regarding Social Issues and Moral Standards of the Evangelical United Brethren Church.[3] A social creed had first entered Methodist history in 1908, when the Methodist Episcopal General Conference adopted one that advocated the abolition of child labor, supported "such regulation of the conditions of labor for women as shall safeguard the physical and moral health of the community," and called for "the highest wage that each industry can afford, and for the most equitable division of the products of industry that can ultimately be devised."[4]

The authors are grateful to Darryl W. Stephens for his contribution to this chapter. He generously made available research on the evolution of the Social Principles 1972–2004, his doctoral dissertation on the Social Principles, two articles he wrote on the central conferences, and two summaries drafted expressly for this chapter. However, decisions concerning the material to be used and judgments about their meaning were made by the authors.

Soon the 1908 Methodist Social Creed, with its emphases on children, women, and economics, found acceptance with the newly established[5] Federal Council of Churches.[6] Because both the Evangelical and the United Brethren churches joined the Federal Council, they came in contact with the Methodist Social Creed, and it influenced their social engagement statements. Between 1908 and the early 1960s, their statements and the Methodist one were revised and expanded periodically. It was the 1964 Methodist *Social Creed* and the 1963 Evangelical United Brethren *Basic Beliefs Regarding Social Issues and Moral Standards* that entered the 1968 United Methodist *Book of Discipline*.

Whereas the Evangelical United Brethren gave more attention to amusements and Sabbath observance and the Methodists more to the economic order, both supported artificial birth control at the very moment, 1968, when Pope Paul VI was reasserting the Roman Catholic ban on artificial contraception. Both statements upheld those who choose to fight for their country and those who refuse for the sake of conscience. Both statements addressed human rights: the Methodist one denounces discrimination based on "race, culture, national origin, social class, or religion. Neither should any person be denied equal political, economic, or legal rights or opportunities because of sex."[7]

Throughout their histories as separate denominations, Evangelicals, United Brethren, and Methodists had leaders who shaped their thinking on those issues and many others—leaders who also believed that the church must lobby influential persons, frequently politicians, to pass laws, such as ones abolishing child labor and protecting working women, to improve society at large. Methodism's founder, John Wesley, did not shy away from speaking truth to power. Writing several times in 1775 to Lord Dartmouth, a key member of King George III's cabinet, Wesley admonished Dartmouth to "speak the truth" to the king, telling him that his country was not prosperous, as the king's other advisers were claiming. Also Wesley urged Dartmouth to warn the king that his rebellious American subjects would not be pushovers: the American rebels, Wesley wrote, would "dispute every inch of ground" with the king's troops.[8]

Wesley devoted less time and energy, however, to stiffening the backbones of politicians than to organizing his Methodist followers to meet individual needs. Methodists fed the hungry; clothed the ragged; gave coal to the shivering; taught the unschooled; visited the sick and imprisoned; and started medical clinics, employment agencies, and loan societies. Wesley personally took up the cause of French prisoners of war who, he thought, were being neglected by his own British government.[9] And during his teaching days at Oxford University, he became, in effect, the defense attorney for a young man accused of homosexual practices, and raised money to pay his fine when he was found guilty.[10]

Wesley's acts of social engagement and his precepts for social reform continue to inform United Methodism's approach to social engagement. His unqualified denunciation of slavery at a time when it was a key part of the British economy sets a high standard: "Give liberty," he insisted, "to every partaker of human nature."[11] But Wesley's practices and precepts are not the last word on any activity or principle. For more than two centuries, Methodists, Evangelicals, and United Brethren have drawn fresh insights for their statements about social issues from biblical studies; the theological discipline of ethics; and such academic fields as history, natural science, economics, and sociology.

Writing United Methodism's Social Principles in a Changing Moral Climate

The most recent part of the history of social thought and practice in the Wesleyan tradition began in 1968, when, as we have seen, the Methodists and the Evangelical United Brethren brought their statements of social engagement to union. The uniting conference ordered their printing back-to-back in the *Discipline*. Then, recognizing the need to have a single statement, it appointed a Social Principles Study Commission, charging it to report to the 1972 General Conference. Its members, chaired by Bishop James S. Thomas, worked during a time when moral and political absolutes were being challenged. One challenge came from historians, who noticed that attempts to write moral absolutes into civil law sometimes come back to bite their advocates. "The future," writes historian Arthur M. Schlesinger Jr., "outwits all our certitudes."[12]

The moral experiment of Prohibition was an example of a crusade to write a moral absolute into civil law that had an unforeseen outcome. During the first two decades of the twentieth century, a majority of Americans decided to fight the evil of drunkenness by prohibiting the making, selling, and drinking of alcoholic beverages. This, they believed, would create a sober country. Shortly after the ban took effect in 1919,[13] it was mugged by consequences. "There were 15,000 saloons in New York when Prohibition started; within a few years, there were 32,000."[14]

Prohibition increased organized crime, handing mobsters the chance to make big bucks supplying bootleg hootch to people dead set on tippling as people had tippled for millennia. Using an amendment to the United States Constitution to fight a moral evil had the consequence, not of producing sober Americans, but of adding a lucrative line of business to organized crime.

While historians were suggesting that prescribing legal remedies for individual and social evils often produces unexpected new evils, situation ethicists were questioning the value of rigid adherence to absolute dos and don'ts. A book mentioned in previous chapters, *Honest to God*, by Bishop J. A. T. Robinson, provides an example of this position: "Nothing can of itself always be labeled as 'wrong.' One cannot, for instance, start from the position 'sex relations before marriage' or 'divorce' are wrong or sinful in themselves. They may be in 99 cases or even 100 cases out of 100, but they are not intrinsically so, for the only intrinsic evil is lack of love."[15] In other words, while absolute dos and don'ts play a vital role in individual and social life, unyielding adherence to them can poison love.

The two challenges to moral and political absolutes just summarized often came together during the 1960s and early 1970s. An example is abortion, which was generally illegal in the United States in the sixties. The consequence of banning abortion was not, however, the elimination of abortions. Rich women traveled to where abortion was legal. Poor women trekked to back-alley abortionists, who often botched their work. So people who thought historically asked: instead of all-out efforts to keep abortion illegal (favored by 85 percent of Americans in 1968[16]) wouldn't it be better to make abortion legal, regulated, and medically safe? Situation ethicists added questions about love: is it loving to force a woman to carry to term a fetus conceived in rape or incest?

Those types of questions asked by historians and situation ethicists, coupled with the culture-shaking forces of the 1960s reviewed in chapter 1, helped change popular opinion. Between 1968 and 1972, the attitude of people in the United States toward abortion evolved dramatically: from 85 percent in favor of keeping abortion illegal to 50 percent supporting legalizing abortion with no limitations, plus an additional 41 percent opting for legalizing abortion under certain conditions.[17] This altered attitude toward abortion symbolizes the cultural climate in which the Social Principles Study Commission worked between 1968 and 1972.

The Social Principles of 1972

After making a preliminary report to the 1970 special General Conference, the Social Principles Study Commission presented draft Social Principles to the 1972 General Conference. These Principles contain seven sections: the Natural World and the Nurturing, Social, Economic, Political, and World communities, and the Social Creed, which sums up the other sections and is designed for unison reading in worship services. Except for the Natural World section, the Principles include carry-over material and new stands. One carryover is: "We reject racism in every form," which is coupled with a new assertion that it is "the obligation of society, and groups within the society, to implement compensatory programs that redress long-standing systematic social deprivation of ethnic minorities."[18]

Strong positions favoring women's rights, contraception, collective bargaining, and the United Nations are carried over, as is traditional opposition to alcoholic beverages, gambling, and capital punishment. Support for nonviolent civil disobedience, which played a pivotal role in the civil rights and antiwar movements of the 1960s, was added in 1972: "Governments, no less than individuals, are subject to the judgment of God. Therefore, we recognize the right of individuals to dissent when acting under the constraint of conscience and, after exhausting all legal recourse, to disobey laws deemed to be unjust."[19]

In continuity with previous statements, war is rejected as incompatible with "the teachings and example of Christ,"[20] which seems to commit the church to pacifism. But the statement goes on to affirm United Methodism's upholding of "persons who conscientiously choose to serve in the armed forces," *and* those "who conscientiously oppose all war, or any particular war,"[21] which implies that Christians can in good conscience support *some* wars—traditionally understood as those wars that meet the criteria for being "just."

Section One of the 1972 Social Principles, "The Natural World," is a new stand, inspired by the mounting environmental movement, initiated by Rachel Carson's 1962 book *Silent Spring* and climaxing in 1970 in the first Earth Day and the establishment of the Environmental Protection Agency. "All creation is the Lord's," the new United Methodist statement reads, "and we are stewards of it. Air, water, soil, minerals, plants, animal life, and space are to be valued and conserved because they are God's creation and not solely because they are useful to human beings."[22]

Abortion entered the 1972 Social Principles in an on-the-one-hand/on-the-other statement: "Our belief in the sanctity of unborn human life makes us reluctant to approve abortion," but we also recognize that "devastating damage" to the mother may be caused by "an unacceptable pregnancy"; therefore "in continuity with past Christian teaching, we recognize tragic conflicts of life with life that may justify abortion," and "we support the removal of abortion from the criminal code."[23] The next year, the U.S. Supreme Court legalized abortion in its *Roe v. Wade* decision authored by Justice Harry A. Blackmun, a United Methodist,[24] who called the decision "a step that had to be taken as we go down the road toward full emancipation of women."[25]

Concerning marriage and divorce, the 1972 Social Principles, appearing at a time when state no-fault divorce laws were being enacted,[26] declare: "We assert the sanctity of the marriage covenant. Marriage between a man and a woman has long been blessed by God and recognized by society." A few sentences later, the paragraph qualifies that statement: "In marriages where the partners are…estranged beyond reconciliation, we recognize divorce and the right of divorced persons to remarry."[27] American society's new occasion of talking openly about the goings-on inside some marriages called for learning a new theological lesson: rethinking the position that marriage is forever. United Methodists concluded officially that divorce is the most loving way to deal with marriages filled with silent indifference, verbal and physical abuse, and spousal rape; unofficially, of course, divorces had been occurring in Methodist, Evangelical, and United Brethren families for many years.

The 1968 uniting conference spoke of homosexuality as a "sexual problem," and argued that those suffering from it should not be discriminated against, nor jailed, but should receive health care and the church's ministry[28]—a statement that reflected the majority opinion of legal and medical professionals in the 1960s. In 1957, however, psychologist Evelyn Hooker had published her groundbreaking study "The Adjustment of the Male Homosexual," in which she reported that her research showed that "homosexuals were not inherently abnormal and that there was no difference between homosexual and heterosexual men in terms of psychology."[29] Hooker's study had no immediate impact on the medical community: the American Psychiatric Association continued to list homosexuality as a mental disorder until 1973. But in 1961, the American Bar Association recommended that laws dealing with private consenting relations between adults be dropped. Homosexuality is not a crime said lawyers. It's a mental illness said psychiatrists, while popular homophobia spouted "fag" jokes and taunts.

A few Methodists, however, were beginning to evaluate the consequences of any stigmatization of gay sexuality, whether as a crime, a mental illness, or a "sexual problem." The Reverend Robert ("Ted") McIlvenna was working with young adults in the neighborhood of Glide Methodist Church in San Francisco when, sometime in 1963, his phone rang. The caller, a gay man, asked Ted to come quickly to a cheap hotel. There he found the man who phoned him and two others, half naked and badly hurt. "Their genitals," McIlvenna recalls, "had been kicked in." Shocked, he asked, "Why haven't you called the police?" "The police have been here. The vice squad. They're the ones who did this." "So why," Ted asked, "haven't you called a doctor?" "A doctor's been here, too. He was disgusted, he didn't want to get involved." In an interview thirty years later, McIlvenna said: "It was a turning point for me. I figured that anyone, no matter what his sexual proclivities, had the basic right of not getting his genitals kicked in by the police."[30]

If a consequence of popular homophobia, coupled with medical and theological opinion, was the brutalization of gay men, then McIlvenna and his fellow Glide Church clergy concluded that as servants of Christ they must take their stand with homosexuals, which they and their wives did at a New Year's Eve gay dance that was raided by the police, even though the organizers had obtained the required permits and the clergy had met in advance with vice squad officers.

Similar social engagement by individuals in a few other places, and the Stonewall Inn riots in 1969 in the Greenwich Village section of New York City that sparked the national "Gay Pride" movement, paved the way for *Motive*, the magazine of United Methodism's student movement, to call, in a 1972 editorial, for thinking in terms of pride, not sickness, about homosexuality: "This issue is for you and for us, Gay men, knowing that in our strength we are proud and glad to be Gay, to be able to love other men, both emotionally and sexually, and knowing that this is beautiful even though our anti-Lesbian/anti-Faggot society denies our existence by dismissing us as 'sick,' and 'misfits.' "[31]

The 1972 General Conference was not ready, however, for gay pride. One of its legislative committees debated this draft statement received from the Social Principles Study Commission: "We declare our acceptance of homosexuals as persons of sacred worth, and we welcome them into the fellowship of the church." The committee retained "sacred worth" but deleted the "welcome." When this revised version reached the floor of General Conference, a phrase—one of the most contentious in the first forty years of United Methodist history—was added: "though we do not condone the practice of homosexuality and consider this practice incompatible with Christian teaching."[32]

The First Post-Watergate Social Principles

The 1976 General Conference was the first one held after Richard Nixon resigned the presidency in 1974 as an outcome of the Watergate break-in and the White House's cover-up. In response, perhaps, this sentence was added to the Social Principles: "National security must not be extended to justify or keep secret maladministration, or illegal and unconscionable activities directed against persons or groups by their own government or by other governments."[33] In the same section of the 1976 Social Principles, a church-state addition appeared: "We believe that the state should not attempt to control the Church, nor should the Church seek to dominate the state. 'Separation of church and state' means no organic union of the two, but does permit interaction. The Church should ... [support] policies and programs deemed to be just and compassionate and [oppose] policies and programs which are not."[34]

Also the 1976 Social Principles signaled United Methodist agreement with several U.S. Supreme Court decisions concerning religious instruction, Bible reading, and prayer in public schools. In *McCollum v. Board of Education* (1948), the Court ruled that religious instruction in public schools violated the U.S. Constitution; in *Engle v. Vitale* (1962), it declared unconstitutional any kind of prayer composed by a public school district, even nondenominational prayer; and in *Abingdon School District v. Schempp* (1963), it banned officially sanctioned Bible reading in public schools. Agreeing with those rulings, the 1976 Social Principles declare that the "state should not use its authority to inculcate particular religious beliefs (including atheism) nor should it require prayer or worship in the public schools, but should leave students free to practice their own religious convictions."[35]

The Sheriffs Ride In

During the 1970s, sheriffs sporting badges identifying them as enforcers of various causes rode onto the American landscape. Some led charges supported by persons from across the religious and political spectrum, such as the antidrug and antichild-pornography movements. Others led assaults on the campaigns for women's rights, abortion rights, and gay rights. When the U.S. Congress passed the Equal Rights Amendment in 1972 ("Equality of rights under the law shall not be denied or abridged by the United States or by any state on account of sex"),[36] Phyllis Schlafly spurred her, ultimately successful,[37] STOP ERA (Stop the Equal Rights Amendment) crusade. The next year, when the Supreme Court legalized abortion in its *Roe v. Wade* decision, both pro-life and pro-choice sheriffs leaped into their saddles. When Dade County, Florida, voted in 1977 to prohibit discrimination on grounds of "affectional or sexual preferences,"[38] Anita Bryant booted up an antigay posse. In 1979, Jerry Falwell founded the Moral Majority and took aim at, among other targets, the Supreme Court's rulings on prayer and Bible-reading in public schools.

As a result of pressure from sheriffs on the right and the left, with significantly heavier pressure coming from the right, United Methodism struggled for much of its forty-year history to define and defend the middle.

Developing United Methodism's Social Principles

Responsibility for developing United Methodism's Social Principles during an era when the middle ground was under attack was assigned by the 1972 General Conference to the newly created General Board of Church and Society, which brought together a number of former Methodist and Evangelical United Brethren social engagement agencies.[39] In the end, however, only General Conference is the United Methodist Church's voice: "No person, no paper, no organization, has the authority to speak officially for The United Methodist Church, this right having been reserved exclusively to the General Conference under the Constitution."[40]

Although the Board of Church and Society has the task of recommending ways to update the Social Principles, others influence the General Conference's decisions by offering their own proposals.

Influencing the Updating of the Social Principles

"Any organization, clergy member, or lay member of the United Methodist Church may petition the General Conference."[41] Thousands of these petitions pour in every four years, are sorted, and then discussed by the appropriate General Conference committees. Many deal with controversial sections of the Social Principles. Between quadrennial General Conferences, the Council of Bishops often addresses social concerns. General boards and agencies, in addition to the Board of Church and Society, issue statements that deal with social engagement. Overseas, United Methodism's central conferences, by means of their translations and adaptations of the Social Principles, contribute to the denomination's store of theological reflection.

The United Methodist Women exert a major influence on the thinking and doing of local-church members and the denomination at large; indeed, the denomination's women may be the single most important influence on the social thinking of United Methodism's laypersons. Leaders of their national organization select social engagement topics and commission books to be used by study groups at the local church, annual conference, and national levels. A sampling of the study-book themes indicates the range of issues considered: "The Welfare Maze" (1974), "Human Rights and the International Order" (1979), "The World's Uprooted" (1983), "Caring for God's Earth" (1985), "Gospel, Culture, and Media" (1990), "Global Economics" (1993), "Restorative Justice" (2002).[42]

Caucuses, which give visibility and voice to an array of groups within United Methodism, put pressure on General Conference delegates to vote the way the caucuses want them to vote. Some of these caucuses represent the church's ethnic communities. Some take up women's concerns. Some attract theological liberals; others appeal to conservatives.

Good News, representing United Methodism's right, devoted considerable time, energy, and money after 1972 to a campaign to make certain that "the practice of homosexuality" would continue to be considered "incompatible with Christian teaching." The caucus's founder, Charles W. Keysor, wrote in 1976: "Should the church abandon its present Biblical stance against homosexual practice, it will precipitate the most divisive climate since the slavery controversy split American Methodism" in the 1840s.[43]

Two caucuses on the left, Affirmation and the Methodist Federation for Social Action, led the opposition to the Good News campaign. Affirmation started life in 1975 as the United Methodist Gay Caucus, which was formed "to insist that our [homosexual] lives and loving are gifts of God, not rebellion against the divine will."[44] The name was changed in 1977 to Affirmation, an organization for lesbian, gay, bisexual, and transgender concerns, "working for more love and justice in the United Methodist Church."[45] After the 1984 General Conference banned the ordination and appointment of "self-avowed practicing homosexuals,"[46] Affirmation created the Reconciling Congregation Program[47] to link local churches seeking to implement "God's imperative for inclusion."[48] Like Affirmation, the Methodist Federation for Social Action lobbies for "the rights of full inclusion of lesbian, gay, bisexual, and transgender persons in the church and society."[49] But the Federation's history is longer and its goals broader than those of Affirmation. Dating to 1907, when it was founded as the Methodist Federation for Social Service, the Federation concerns itself with "issues of justice, peace, and liberation."[50]

Other Social Conscience Voices

United Methodist bishops lack authorization, either individually or collectively, to speak *for* the church, but when the Council of Bishops exercises its mandate to speak *to* "the Church and from the Church to the world,"[51] what it says carries considerable weight. Perhaps the bishops' most resounding pastoral letter came in 1986. Titled "In Defense of Creation: The Nuclear Crisis and a Just Peace," the letter said that the bishops had been reflecting "on the continuing build-up of nuclear arsenals" and "the devastation that such weapons can inflict on planet Earth.... Therefore, we say a clear and unconditional *No* to nuclear war and to any use of nuclear weapons.... We state our complete lack of confidence in proposed 'defenses' against nuclear attack [the Reagan administration's 'Star Wars' missile defense proposal] and are convinced that the enormous cost of developing such defenses is one more witness to the obvious fact that the arms race is a social justice issue, not only a war and peace issue."[52]

In 1995, the bishops opened a churchwide initiative on children and poverty. Six years later, they renewed it by issuing a pastoral letter titled "Community with Children and the Poor." "The crisis among children and the impoverished continues unabated as we enter a new millennium," the bishops said. In the United States, "more than 25 percent of U.S. children live in poverty, the highest rate among industrialized nations." The self-centered values of "American individualism and capitalism," the bishops warned, infect church and society alike. To counter these values, they urged United Methodists to evaluate "everything the church is and does in the light of their impact on children and the impoverished."[53]

On February 6, 2003, a month before President George W. Bush ordered the invasion of Iraq, the president of the Council of Bishops, Sharon Brown Christopher, sent a pastoral letter to Mr. Bush, a United Methodist, saying: "The human community stands at an intersection of decision that will shape its common life and international relations for years to come. In your hands rests in large part the path we will follow."[54]

Various statements of the Council of Bishops (pastoral letters, episcopal addresses to General Conference, and sermons by individual bishops) have been collected by Bishops James Mathews and William Oden in *Vision and Supervision: A Sourcebook of Significant Documents of the Council of Bishops of The United Methodist Church.*[55]

In addition to the social conscience voice raised by the Council of Bishops, United Methodism's overseas central conferences address social issues. Annual conferences outside the United States are organized into seven central conferences: Africa, Central and Southern Europe, Congo, Germany, Northern Europe, Philippines, and West Africa.[56] The church's Constitution grants these conferences authority to make "such changes and adaptations of the [General Conference-approved *Discipline*] as the conditions in the respective areas may require."[57] Exercising this power, central conferences translate the Social Principles into the languages of their regions and adapt them to the cultures in which they work.

Participants in a consultation held in Vienna, Austria, in March 2006 lamented the way United Methodism's Social Principles are dominated by U.S.-American experiences and American English usage.[58] In spite of this concern, most central conferences, committed as they are to United Methodist connectionalism, content themselves with translating the Social Principles into the principal language spoken in their area, embracing "the vast majority of the text without alteration,"[59] with adaptations "expressed through small additions or deletions of text, alteration of single words or phrases, and rearrangement of word order."[60]

The Africa Central Conference,[61] while providing a reference to the denomination's Social Principles, published its own "Special Advices" in its *Le Livre Discipline* (1990).[62] Under five headings—Christian Stewardship, Entertainment, Temperance, Marriage, and Tribalism—the "Advices" adapt American Methodist teachings from the 1930s to the Africa scene in the late twentieth century.[63] "Christian marriage" is distinguished from other kinds of marriage; for example, "mixed marriage" between a Christian and a non-Christian. Responsibility for setting the grounds for granting a divorce is assigned to the state, but the "Advices" establish the justifiable grounds for a divorce if a person is to be remarried by a United Methodist pastor; namely childlessness, adultery, and cruelty.[64] Although the "Advices" do not deal with polygamy, the Africa Central Conference, yielding to cultural reality, allows polygamous persons to join the church.[65] Homosexuality is not mentioned, but the African Central Conference told the 2000 General Conference that its understanding of Christianity and "African traditional culture"[66] calls for total opposition to the homosexual lifestyle, same-sex marriages and civil unions, and the ordination and appointment of homosexual clergy.[67]

In Europe, the Germany Central Conference's adaptation of United Methodism's Social Principles seems to provide for affirming sexual relations outside of marriage. The denominational statement declares that "sexual relations are only clearly affirmed in the marriage bond."[68] For "the marriage bond," German United Methodists substituted "einer verbindlichen Partnerschaft," which Darryl Stephens translates as "a binding partnership."[69] This substitution appears to allow German United Methodists to affirm couples who live together monogamously without marrying.

Regularly Updated Documents

Some of the social engagement materials just discussed are easy to locate; others are not. Every four years, after each General Conference, an updated version of the Social Principles appears in the new *Book of Discipline*. Many General Conference actions related to social engagement are not incorporated in the Social Principles, however. Principal among these are resolutions that are applications to particular situations of the basic guidelines set forth in the Principles. These resolutions are published, simultaneously with each new *Discipline*, in an updated *Book of Resolutions*, which contains new resolutions and previous ones that are still in effect. In contrast with the ease of finding the books of *Discipline* and *Resolutions*, one must search differently formatted United Methodist websites in order to pull up the social engagement statements of the church's boards, agencies, and caucuses; and the *Disciplines* of the central conferences are available, for the most part, only in libraries on the continents where they were published.

A sampling of resolution titles from various editions of the *Book of Resolutions*, which ballooned from 448 pages in 1984 to 954 in 2004, gives some indication of the range of subjects covered: "Social Welfare" (1968), "Investment Ethics" (1972), "Gun Control" (1976), "Juvenile Justice" (1980), "The Arab-Israeli Conflict" (1984), "Available and Affordable Housing" (1992), and "Call for a Rebirth of Compassion" (1996). Such topics as "AIDS and the Healing Ministry of the Church" (1988), "Human Cloning" (2000), and "Plan to Eliminate Terrorism" (2004) reveal United Methodism responding to developments in the world at large. In like manner, the Social Principles continued to develop.

Evolving Social Principles, 1980–2004

Successive General Conferences expanded the scope of the Social Principles and defined their role. The 1980 definition says they "are intended to be instructive and persuasive in the best of the prophetic spirit,"[70] which implies that strict adherence is not mandatory. Expanding the Principles, the 1980 General Conference inserted an affirmation of the "importance of women in decision-making positions at all levels of church life,"[71] a challenge to the "selfish spirit which often pervades our economic life,"[72] and a condemnation of "the production, possession, or use of nuclear weapons."[73]

When the 1984 General Conference declared that "the Church regards the institution of slavery as an infamous evil,"[74] perhaps it was remembering that the 1784 founding conference of American Methodism had called for extirpating the "Abomination" of slavery. Or perhaps it was recognizing that forms of slavery still exist. Whatever the reason for adding the censure of slavery in 1984, it is interesting to observe that the organizers of Methodism in the United States rooted their condemnation of slavery in "the Golden Law of God" (Scripture) *and* "the unalienable[75] Rights of Mankind" (rights discerned by reason and articulated by Thomas Jefferson in the Declaration of Independence).[76] Darryl Stephens notes the same rooting of the current Principles: "Theologically, the [Principles'] commitments to civil, political, and human rights share much in common with…the 'American Creed,'" which "asserts the ideals of freedom, democracy, equality, liberty, certain inalienable rights, and 'the essential dignity of the individual human being.' "[77]

The 1988 Social Principles called The United Methodist Church "to take the leadership role in bringing together [the medical, theological, and social science] disciplines to address this most complex issue"— human sexuality.[78] Concerning homosexuality, the italicized portion of this sentence is new: "Although we do not condone the practice of homosexuality and consider this practice incompatible with Christian teaching, *we affirm that God's grace is available to all. We commit ourselves to be in ministry for and with all persons.*"[79]

In 2000, the statement on war in the Social Principles was, significantly, revised. Whereas the 1988 statement, coming on the heels of the Council of Bishops' 1986 letter "In Defense of Creation," offered no justification for war,[80] the 2000 statement acknowledged "that most Christians regretfully realize that, when peaceful alternatives have failed, the force of arms may be preferable to unchecked aggression, tyranny and genocide." We "respect those who support the use of force, but only in extreme situations and only when the need is clear beyond reasonable doubt, and through appropriate international organizations."[81] The 2000 Principles qualified the 1988 ones in another place: the 1988 Principles declared: "We believe war is incompatible with the teachings and example of Christ. We therefore reject war as an instrument of national foreign policy";[82] the 2000 Principles retained those sentences, but inserted *usual* between "an" and "instrument," thereby deleting the implied pacifism of the 1988 declaration.[83]

Good News Magazine, in the wake of 9/11 and the U.S. attack on Afghanistan, carried an article by James V. Heidinger titled "Using Force to Overcome Evil." Heidinger selected the new material in the 2000 Social Principles to support the use of violence to "defend the defenseless, protect the innocent, and promote justice." In a letter to the magazine, Roger Wolsey worried about Heidinger's use of the new position on war, saying that he doubted that the Gulf War of 1991 and the post-9/11 War on Terror were really about defending the defenseless, protecting the innocent, and promoting justice. Rather, he suggested, they were about forcibly maintaining "the unjust situation where two-thirds of the world's resources are being consumed by five percent of the world's population (United States)."[84]

The differences between the statements on war in the 1988 and 2000 Social Principles reveal how world events and shifting voting majorities in the General Conference tend to alter United Methodism's theological stance on various issues. And the exchange of views between Heidinger and Wolsey reveal how words and concepts in the *Discipline* can be interpreted diversely. Because they disagreed on how to define the cause being fought for, they disagreed on whether the war being fought met the 2000 *Discipline*'s standard of using force "only in extreme situations and only when the need is clear beyond reasonable doubt."[85]

Just as Wolsey and Heidinger were responding to front-page news, so do new Social Principles' sections show United Methodism tracking headline-nabbing issues: 1992—Science and Technology, Rights of Homosexual Persons, Adoption, Media Violence and Christian Values;[86] 1996—Family Violence and Abuse, Sexual Harassment, Right to Health Care, Organ Transplantation and Donation;[87] 2000—Food Safety, Suicide, Sustainable Agriculture, The Internet, Persons Living with HIV and AIDS, Family Farms, Corporate Responsibility;[88] 2004—Ministry to Those Who Have Experienced an Abortion, Trade and Investment.

As those sections were being added, a strong cultural wind was blowing toward the political and religious right. Sometimes this wind drove United Methodism in a rightward direction. Sometimes the church pushed leftward against the prevailing wind. Usually it dug in its heels on middle ground. A paragraph on adoption[89] inserted in 1992 just below the one on abortion may be read as affirmation of adoption and opposition to abortion; this reading finds support in a 2004 insert in the abortion material: "We particularly encourage the church, the government, and social service agencies to support and facilitate the option of adoption."[90] The 2000 General Conference opposed "the use of late-term abortion known as dilation and extraction (partial-birth abortion)."[91] Whereas the modifications indicate antiabortion pressure from the right, United Methodism held firmly to its 1972 recognition that "tragic conflicts of life with life may justify abortion,"[92] and the church took a strong stand in 1996 against abortion-protest violence: "We do not encourage or condone, under any circumstances, any form of violent protest or action against anyone involved in the abortion dilemma."[93]

United Methodism refused to back off from its declaration that the practice of homosexuality is incompatible with Christian teaching, yet it simultaneously expanded its call for recognizing the civil rights of gay men and lesbians. A 1988 insertion insists "that all persons, regardless of age, gender, marital status, or sexual orientation, are entitled to have their human and civil rights ensured."[94] That sentence became a new paragraph in 1992: "We are committed to support [basic human rights and civil liberties] for homosexual persons. We see a clear issue of simple justice in protecting their rightful claims where they have: shared material resources, pensions, guardian relationships, mutual powers of attorney, and other...lawful claims typically attendant to contractual relationships....Moreover, we support efforts to stop violence and other forms of coercion against gays and lesbians."[95]

The 1996 General Conference decreed that ceremonies celebrating "homosexual unions shall not be conducted by our ministers and shall not be conducted in our churches";[96] this prohibition was moved to a different section of the *Discipline* in 2000 to make certain that United Methodist clergy could be tried and lose their clergy rights for disobeying it.[97] The 2000 General Conference implored "families and churches not to reject or condemn their lesbian and gay members and friends."[98] This positive action was challenged, however, when the church's Judicial Council ruled in 2005 that a Virginia Conference pastor could refuse to accept a practicing gay man into the membership of his church.[99] The 2004 Social Principles "support laws in civil society that define marriage as the union of one man and one woman."[100] This leaves the question of "civil unions" unaddressed, although the statement about civil rights and liberties added in 1992 (quoted above) may be read as openness to civil "unions" as distinguished from civil "marriages."

An example of United Methodism tacking leftward against the cultural wind blowing toward the right is its opposition to capital punishment. The Methodist Church first spoke out against the death penalty in 1952, prior to any other major U.S. Protestant denomination and the Roman Catholic Church. Beginning in 1972, resistance to the death penalty was included in one paragraph or another in the Political Community section of the Social Principles. The majority of Americans, however, continued to support the U.S. Supreme Court's 1976 *Gregg v. Georgia* decision that the death penalty is not in itself a "cruel and unusual" punishment prohibited by the Constitution; therefore it is constitutional to execute persons convicted of certain clearly defined crimes. Refusing to bow to public opinion,[101] the 2004 Social Principles turned United Methodism's longstanding opposition to capital punishment into a paragraph of its own: "We believe the death penalty denies the power of Christ to redeem, restore and transform all human beings....When governments implement the death penalty (capital punishment), then the life of the convicted person is devalued and all possibility of change in that person's life ends.... For this reason, we oppose the death penalty (capital punishment) and urge its elimination from all criminal codes."[102]

United Methodism steered a middle course during a time when right-wingers were pitting the Bible against the scientific theory of evolution. The church added a section on science and technology to its Social Principles in 1992: "Concerning that which science has offered the world, facts alone can be empty and confusing without an integrating interpretation best accomplished through dialogue with the scientific community."[103] This statement was revised four years later as antievolution forces ramped up their crusade: "We recognize science as a legitimate interpretation of God's natural world. We affirm the validity of the claims of science in describing the natural world, although we preclude science from making authoritative claims about theological issues.... Science and theology are complementary rather than mutually incompatible. We therefore encourage dialogue between the scientific and theological communities."[104]

While successive General Conferences were expanding the Social Principles, United Methodist congregations were giving feet and hands to some of the Principles' core concerns.

From Bethlehem to Rwanda, from Lawyers' Row to Prison, and Sanctuary in Tacoma and Chicago

Local churches in the five jurisdictions in the United States and the central conferences in Africa, Europe, and the Philippines inspire their members to participate in love and justice projects at home and around the globe. The following stories are four examples of what thousands of congregations are doing.

The administrative council of First Church, Tacoma, Washington, approved the opening of the church's doors on June 17, 2006, as a place of refuge for service men and women who could not in good conscience fight in Iraq. This offer of sanctuary responded to First Lieutenant Ehren Watada's attempt to resign his commission because of his belief that "the war in Iraq is illegal." The congregation's pastor, Monty Smith, "said the church stands 'in solidarity' with others who hold similar social-justice convictions."[105]

The congregation of Wesley Church, Bethlehem, Pennsylvania, responding to Senior Pastor William Lentz's challenge, underwrote a two-week mission to Rwanda in 2005. The mission's medical team—an emergency room physician, a nurse practitioner, and an infectious diseases nurse—treated 600 patients, mostly women and children, for AIDS, various infections, river blindness, and gynecological problems. Two vacation Bible schools, one in the suburbs of Kigali, the other in a rural area, were staffed by a certified music teacher, a Christian education specialist, and an early-childhood educator. Lentz, assisted by a retired Presbyterian minister from Wesley Church's staff and an ordained United Methodist who is a citizen of Zimbabwe, conducted a pastors' licensing school, providing classes in general Bible study, preaching, church history, and United Methodist history, doctrine, and polity for fifty-four persons who were then licensed by the bishop of the East Africa Annual Conference. The money raised, $60,000, paid the expenses of the eleven missioners; provided supplies, including mattresses, pillows, and blankets for the pastors' school; purchased antibiotics, pain relievers, and mosquito netting for distribution by the medical team; and bought arts and crafts material for the Bible schools.[106]

In Chicago, Adalberto Memorial Church extended sanctuary in 2006 to Elvira Arellano, the congregation's lay leader and the president of La Familia Latina Unida, which was pressing President George W. Bush to place a moratorium on deporting undocumented immigrants until Congress approved reforms. Mrs. Arellano, facing deportation, was first arrested in 2003 for using a fake Social Security card to work in the United States in order to care for her son, a U.S. citizen, who has health problems. Bishop Minerva Carcaño (Phoenix Area) and Bishop Hee-soo Jung (Chicago Area) visited Mrs. Arellano in her sanctuary.[107]

First Church, Lancaster, Pennsylvania, faces Duke Street, the city's traditional lawyers' row. From that base, guided by Senior Pastor Kent Kroehler, members of the church staff and lay volunteers go out to five prisons to visit members and nonmembers; men and women receive post-incarceration support; and church members, implementing the Social Principles, are advocates for ending the death penalty. For two years after Hurricane Katrina devastated New Orleans in 2005, bi-monthly work teams of ten to thirty-five youths and adults traveled there to rehabilitate homes, provide vacation Bible schools, and support local public schools. The congregation has one third of its members involved in various servant ministries and raised about $45,000 for post-tsunami and post-Katrina relief. They assist annual teams of fifteen to twenty persons to fly to Bluefields, Nicaragua, where they built a school for 300 children, a small water system, and an Internet café. Also in Bluefields, they fund teachers and supplies, finance a medical clinic and nurse, and conduct an annual Bible school. Back in Lancaster, church members offer a cold-weather men's shelter, prepare and serve meals at city shelters, and provide space for a multichurch food bank.[108]

A New Social Creed

Methodism's first Social Creed was approved, as we have seen, by the 1908 General Conference. To celebrate the Creed's centennial, the General Board of Church and Society set up a Social Creed Task Force to draft a new one. In May 2006 Bishop Susan Morrison, a member of the drafting task force, spoke about the writers' desire to create a contemporary, memorable, and singable Social Creed: "We wanted to rewrite the creed for the new generation. We wanted to make it memorable so it would inform young people about their faith in language they use."[109] The Task Force's proposed Creed was approved by the board in October 2006, and was discussed at conferences in Africa, the Philippines, and Europe in 2007.[110] The final draft will be submitted to the 2008 General Conference.

While the first Creed bypassed theology and dealt almost exclusively with economic issues, the proposed one is trinitarian in language and broader in scope:[111]

> God in the Spirit revealed in Jesus Christ,
> calls us by grace
>> *to be renewed in the image of our Creator,*
>> *that we may be one*
>> *in divine love for the world.*

> Today is the day
> God cares for the integrity of creation,
>> wills the healing and wholeness of all life,
>> weeps at the plunder of earth's goodness.
> *And so shall we.*

> Today is the day
> God embraces all hues of humanity,
>> delights in diversity and difference,

favors solidarity transforming strangers into friends.
And so shall we.

Today is the day
God cries with the masses of starving people,
  despises growing disparity between rich and poor,
  demands justice for workers in the marketplace.
And so shall we.

Today is the day
God deplores violence in our homes and streets,
  rebukes the world's warring madness,
  humbles the powerful and lifts up the lowly.
And so shall we.

Today is the day
God calls for nations and peoples to live in peace,
  celebrates where justice and mercy embrace,
  exults when the wolf grazes with the lamb.
And so shall we.

Today is the day
God brings good news to the poor,
  proclaims release to the captives,
  gives sight to the blind, and
  sets the oppressed free.
And so shall we.[112]

In the fall of 2006, the General Board of Church and Society requested proposals for setting the draft Social Creed to music; submissions came in slowly, with more expected from the meetings in Europe, the Philippines, and Africa in 2007.[113] It was hoped that the proposed Creed could "be set to rap, African, country and many other musical beats."[114]

New Occasions. New Lessons?

At the beginning of this chapter, we suggested that debates about statements of social engagement nudge United Methodists to consider new theological lessons. The narrative in this chapter indicates that sometimes this happened, sometimes it did not. United Methodism's position on abortion was stated in 1972 and revised by later General Conferences, all without any churchwide debate about how the church's doctrinal statements and its official way of doing theology (using Scripture, tradition, experience, and reason) undergird the original statement and its modified successors. The historian gets the impression that changing General Conference voting majorities had more to do with the development of the church's position on abortion than did new occasions challenging the church to entertain new theological insights. This impression may be strengthened by the fact that United Methodists are anti-capital punishment and, with a number of qualifications, pro-choice on abortion—a combination that seems to call for a theological debate. Yet it did not occur.

The issue of homosexuality did, however, cause the church to pick up some theological homework. The 1992 report of the Committee to Study Homosexuality, by specifying what the church, using the Bible, cannot teach, dealt with the United Methodist affirmation that Scripture is primary:

> The church cannot teach that the Bible is indifferent to homosexual acts. Although there are only a few passages where such are in view, in every one of those passages a negative judgment about homosexual practice is either stated or presumed. The church cannot teach that all biblical references and allusions to sexual practices are binding today just because they are in the Bible. Specific references and allusions must be examined in light of the basic biblical witness and their respective socio-cultural contexts.[115]

That theological approach to biblical interpretation was *received* by the 1992 General Conference, but not adopted. And homosexuality continued to be United Methodism's most potentially divisive issue, with the result that a Diversity Dialogue Team was selected by the General Commission on Christian Unity and Interreligious Concerns. Recognizing the possibility of schism over the practice of homosexuality, the Team noted, when it released its report in 1998, the presence of *compatibilists* and *incompatibilists* within the church: "Compatibilists believe that both sides on the issues of the morality of homosexual behavior and the nature and status of divine revelation can be held together within the same denomination. . . . Incompatibilists do not believe that these divergent judgments can be housed indefinitely within the same denomination." Then, in effect, the Team called for finding a way to hold compatibilists and incompatibilists together, and recommended "the reading of the writings of John Wesley as they relate to the topic of unity."[116]

The next year, a consultation was held on "Scriptural Authority and the Nature of God's Revelation," a theme that called for digging around the roots of the theological differences among United Methodists. At those roots are clashing opinions about whether the experiences and concepts of ancient cultures that make up the Bible's narratives are part of the abiding Word of God for our day, or whether they must be sieved out in order to hear God's abiding Word for contemporary women and men.

Although the consultation on "Scriptural Authority" and the previous studies did not end United Methodism's debate about the practice of homosexuality, they did produce documents that show United Methodists using that practice's threat to their unity to reconsider their theology of biblical authority and to seek an expression of core beliefs that would hold compatibilists and incompatibilists together in Christian love.

As United Methodism approached age forty, it continued to seek ways to discover and occupy middle ground.

Conclusion

In late 2006 and early in 2007, there were signs that middle ground was regaining favor in the United States. Commentators on the November 2006 U.S. elections noted that voters had tended to opt for centrist Democrats and to oust Republicans who were seen as leaning too far to the right. Two prominent United Methodists, Ted Strickland and Bob Edgar, took public stands on centrist values in 2006. Strickland won the governorship of Ohio on a platform emphasizing the moral issues of poverty and the environment. "We changed the conversation about moral values," one of Strickland's advisers said. "It was impossible for it to be only about abortion and gay marriage."[117] Edgar, general secretary of the National Council of Churches, published a book titled *Middle Church: Reclaiming the Moral Values of the Faithful Majority from the Religious Right.* "I hope this book helps ... move us," Edgar writes, "beyond private piety issues like abortion, homosexuality, and civil marriage to the more important fundamental moral values of ending poverty, healing a broken planet, and seeking nonviolent and peaceful solutions to the world's global conflicts."[118] Edgar goes on to explain that he uses "Middle

Church" as "an umbrella term ... to refer to mainstream people of all faiths," Jews and Muslims as well as Christians.[119] For Christians: "The classic, historical Christianity practiced by Middle Church is far more authentic than the narrow religious expression of most radical right-wing religious leaders."[120]

United Methodism has tried to live in an always shifting, never clearly defined center. Now, as the church nears age forty, there is evidence of movement, at least in the United States, toward similar ground on social and political issues. Perhaps United Methodism's traditional centrism belongs to the future as well as the past.

For further reading, see the Social Principles in the current *Book of Discipline of The United Methodist Church* and the resolutions in the current *Book of Resolutions of The United Methodist Church*; the resolutions are organized under the section headings used by the Social Principles: Natural World, Nurturing Community, Social Community, Economic Community, Political Community, and World Community.

NOTES

Chapter 1: Historical Roots of United Methodism's Union

1. The story of the development of American Methodism is briefly told in John G. McEllhenney, ed., *United Methodism in America: A Compact History* (Nashville: Abingdon Press, 1992).

2. The most recent and complete history of the Evangelical United Brethren Church is J. Bruce Behney and Paul H. Eller, *The History of the Evangelical United Brethren Church* (Nashville: Abingdon Press, 1979).

3. See Terry M. Heisey, ed., *Evangelical from the Beginning: A History of the Evangelical Congregational Church and Its Predecessors* (Lexington, Ky.: Emeth Press, 2006).

4. For example, Elmer T. Clark et al., eds., *The Journal and Letters of Francis Asbury* (Nashville: Abingdon Press, 1958), I:115, 152-53, 190, 549, 657; II:128, 440; III:333.

5. Behney and Eller, 103. See also, Abram W. Sangrey, ed., *Christian Newcomer: His Life and Journal* (reprint, Lancaster, Pa.: Brenneman Printing, 1996), 220.

6. Clark, II:753-54. Ironically, a footnote in this entry observes, "A regrettable action of the conference was the breaking off of negotiations for a merger with the United Brethren Church."

7. Henry Boehm, *Reminiscences, Historical and Biographical, of Sixty-four Years in the Ministry* (New York: Carlton & Porter, 1866).

8. Behney and Eller, 54.

9. See also Jeffery P. Mickle, "A Comparison of the Doctrine of Ministry of Francis Asbury and Philip William Otterbein," in Russell E. Richey, Kenneth E. Rowe, and Jean Miller Schmidt, eds., *Perspectives on American Methodism* (Nashville: Abingdon Press, 1993) as well as Behney and Eller, 106-7.

10. Behney and Eller, 71.

11. Ibid., 78.

Chapter 2: Overview and Context

In these notes and throughout this book *The Book of Discipline of The United Methodist Church* is abbreviated as *BODUMC* with the appropriate date. All references in *BODUMC* are to page numbers rather than to paragraphs.

1. Nolan B. Harmon, ed., *The Encyclopedia of World Methodism*, vol. 2 (Nashville: United Methodist Publishing House, 1974), 1864–65.

2. Andrew Hussey, *Paris: The Secret History* (New York: Bloomsbury, 2007), 416.

3. For details of the student rebellion of May 1968, see ibid., 409-16.

4. Russell E. Richey, Kenneth E. Rowe, and Jean Miller Schmidt, eds., *The Methodist Experience in America: A Sourcebook* (Nashville: Abingdon Press, 2000), II:616.

5. http://www.africanonline.com/reports_kerner.htm (accessed August 10, 2006).

6. *BODUMC*, 1968, 36.

7. Earl D. C. Brewer, *Continuation or Transformation? The Involvement of United Methodism in Social Movements and Issues* (Nashville: Abingdon Press, 1982), 53.

8. *BODUMC*, 2004, 24, 31.

9. *BODUMC*, 2004, 83.

10. Philip Jenkins, *Decade of Nightmares: The End of the Sixties and the Making of Eighties America* (New York: Oxford University Press, 2006), 19.

11. Lizette Alvarez, "Gay Groups Renew Drive Against 'Don't Ask, Don't Tell,'" *New York Times*, September 14, 2006.

12. *BODUMC*, 2004, 120.

13. "The policy, grounded in a belief that open homosexuality is damaging to unit morale and cohesion, stipulates that gay men and lesbians must serve in silence and refrain from homosexual activity, and that recruiters and commanders may not ask them about their sexual orientation in the absence of compelling evidence that homosexual acts have occurred" (Alvarez, *New York Times*, September 14, 2006).

14. *BORUMC*, 2004, 179, Resolution 49, "Homosexuals in the Military." "A Gallop poll in 2004 found that 63 percent of respondents favored allowing gay troops to serve openly, and a similar survey, by the Pew Research Center this year, put the number at 60 percent; those majorities did not exist in 1993. Young people in particular now have more tolerant views about homosexuality" (Alvarez, *New York Times*, September 14, 2006).

15. See Francis S. Collins, *The Language of God: A Scientist Presents Evidence for Belief* (New York: Free Press, 2006), 159-61.

16. *BODUMC*, 1972, 86.

17. Richey, Rowe, and Miller Schmidt, II:618.

18. http://www.zero-nukes.org/defenseofcreation.pdf (accessed August 10, 2006).

19. Jenkins, 219-21.

20. http://www.goodnewsmag.org/renewal/houston_declaration.htm (accessed July 17, 2006).

21. The Council of Bishops of The United Methodist Church, *Vital Congregations—Faithful Disciples* (Nashville: Graded Press, 1990).

22. *BODUMC*, 1992, 91.

23. http://confessingumc.org/v2/resources/confession.htm (accessed July 28, 2006).

24. See "Nebraska Pastor Jimmy Creech Defends 'Holy Unions' of Same-Sex Couples," "Bishops Issue Pastoral Statement on 'Holy Unions' and Homosexuality," and "Judicial Council Determines Disciplinary Prohibition Against Homosexual Unions Enforceable," in Richey, Rowe, and Miller Schmidt, II:687-98.

25. http://www.confessingumc.org/indianapolis_affirmation.html (accessed July 10, 2006).

26. *BODUMC*, 2004, 719, ¶2702:1.b.

27. Neela Banerjee, "Clergywomen Find Hard Path to Bigger Pulpit," *New York Times,* August 26, 2006.

28. Ian Urbina, "An Old World Close to a New World Horror," *New York Times,* October 6, 2006.

29. "Billanthropy" and "The new powers in giving," *The Economist,* July 1, 2006, 9, 63-65.

30. "Middle America's soul: If you want to understand America, turn that dial to a country-music station," *The Economist,* December 23, 2006, 45-46.

31. "Middle America's soul," 46.

32. "Dixie Chicks," accessed at http://en.wikipedia.org/wiki/Dixie_Chicks (accessed March 1, 2007).

33. David Hare, *Stuff Happens* (New York: Faber & Faber, 2004), 93.

34. "9/11/06," *New York Times,* September 11, 2006.

35. "Declassified Key Judgments of the National Intelligence Estimate on Global Terrorism," *New York Times,* September 27, 2006.

36. "Can America's most famous mayor become the Republican Party's champion?" *The Economist,* February 10, 2007, 34.

37. Sermon 92, "On Zeal," §1; *The Works of John Wesley* (Bicentennial Edition), vol. 3, (Nashville: Abingdon Press, 1986), 309.

38. American historian Arthur Schlesinger Jr. selected *The Vital Center* as the title for one of his books.

Chapter 3: Connection

1. *BODUMC,* 2004, 90.

2. Susan R. Howdle, "Connexionalism," in John A. Vickers, ed., *A Dictionary of Methodism in Britain and Ireland* (Peterborough, U.K.: Epworth, 2000), 77.

3. *Minutes of the Methodist Conferences, Annually Held in America: From 1773 to 1813, Inclusive* (New York: Hitt & Wall, 1813; reprint, Swainsboro, Ga.: Magnolia Press, 1983), 5.

4. See, for example, Russell E. Richey, Dennis M. Campbell, and William B. Lawrence, *Marks of Methodism: Theology in Ecclesial Practice,* United Methodism and American Culture, vol. 5 (Nashville: Abingdon Press, 2005), 17-40.

5. Evangelical United Brethren General Conference *Minutes,* 1958, 405, 481.

6. Evangelical United Brethren General Conference *Minutes,* 1966, 372.

7. *Church and Home,* IV (September 1967), 36.

8. J. Bruce Behney and Paul H. Eller, *The History of the Evangelical United Brethren Church* (Nashville: Abingdon Press, 1979), 391.

9. Russell E. Richey, Kenneth E. Rowe, and Jean Miller Schmidt, eds., *The Methodist Experience in America: A Sourcebook* (Nashville: Abingdon Press, 2000), II:616.

10. Richey, Rowe, and Miller Schmidt, II:605.

11. *BODUMC,* 1968, 22. See also *BODUMC,* 1968, 152-53, 157-58.

12. *BODUMC,* 1968, 18.

13. *BODUMC,* 1968, 27-28.

14. *BODUMC,* 1968, 20.

15. *BODUMC*, 1968, 455-57.

16. *BODUMC*, 1968, 437.

17. *BODUMC*, 1968, 202ff.

18. *Discipline of The Evangelical United Brethren Church* (Dayton, Ohio: The Board of Publication of The Evangelical United Brethren Church, 1967), 126ff, 180-81, 222. Hereafter referred to as *DEUBC*.

19. See *Doctrines and Discipline of The Methodist Church* (Nashville: Methodist Publishing House, 1964), 664-91. Hereafter referred to as *DDMC*.

20. *Church and Home*, V (February 1968), 28. See also Theodore R. Buzzard, *Lest We Forget: A History of the Evangelical United Brethren in the Pacific Northwest* (Portland, Oreg., 1988). This church is now the Evangelical Church. See Eileen W. Lindner, ed., *Yearbook of American and Canadian Churches, 2002* (Nashville: Abingdon Press, 2002), 103.

21. *Journal of the 1972 General Conference of The United Methodist Church*, II:1942.

22. Ibid., 1967.

23. Ibid., 1947.

24. Ibid., 1956-66.

25. Ibid., 1951.

26. *BODUMC*, 1968, 82-104.

27. *BODUMC*, 1980, 126.

28. *BODUMC*, 1996, 137.

29. See the *BODUMC*, 1968, 535-37, which contains an index listing annual conference agencies.

30. *BODUMC*, 1996, 369.

31. *Daily Christian Advocate, Advance Edition, 2000 General Conference* (Nashville: United Methodist Publishing House, 2000), I:10.

32. Ibid., I:10-13.

33. Ibid., I:18-20.

34. *BODUMC*, 2004, 508-12.

35. *BODUMC*, 1968, 17.

36. James S. Thomas, *Methodism's Racial Dilemma: The Story of the Central Jurisdiction* (Nashville: Abingdon Press, 1992), 132. This is an important historical study of the Central Jurisdiction by one who participated in its life from 1939 to 1968. Efforts have been mounted to maintain the historical importance of the Central Jurisdiction. See Barbara Ricks Thompson, ed., *The Central Jurisdiction Recovery Project: Preserving Our Past . . . Building Our Future . . .* (Washington, D.C.: General Commission on Religion and Race, 2006).

37. Grant S. Shockley, ed., *Heritage and Hope: The African-American Presence in United Methodism* (Nashville: Abingdon Press, 1991), 372. This volume gives an extensive history of African Americans in American Methodism. See also Richey, Rowe, and Schmidt, II: 611-13, 635-40.

38. See Richey, Rowe, and Miller Schmidt, II:643-44, 658-61.

39. For the historic role of Hispanics in United Methodism see Justo L. González, *Each in Our Own Tongue: A History of Hispanic United Methodism* (Nashville: Abingdon Press, 1991). See also Richey, Rowe, and Miller Schmidt, II:620-21, 645-52.

40. Artemio R. Guillermo, *Churches Aflame: Asian Americans and United Methodism* (Nashville: Abingdon Press, 1991), 142. Guillermo includes a detailed description of NFAAUM meetings from 1970 through 1985.

41. Ibid., 143.

42. Richey, Rowe, and Miller Schmidt, II:631.

43. Thomas E. Frank, *Polity, Practice, and the Mission of The United Methodist Church* (Nashville: Abingdon Press, 2006), 260. The first clergy women, ten in number, were seated at the 1976 General Conference.

44. For a brief history of the Methodist Federation for Social Action, see George D. McClain, "Pioneering Social Gospel Radicalism: An Overview of the History of the Methodist Federation for Social Action," in Russell E. Richey, Kenneth E. Rowe, and Jean Miller Schmidt, eds., *Perspectives on American Methodism: Interpretive Essays* (Nashville: Kingswood Books, 1993), 371-85.

45. For a comprehensive history of Good News, see Riley B. Case, *Evangelical and Methodist: A Popular History* (Nashville: Abingdon Press, 2004). For a critique of Good News and related organizations, see Leon Howell, *United Methodist @ Risk: A Wake-Up Call* (Kingston, N.Y.: Information Project for United Methodists, 2003).

46. *The 2005 United Methodist Directory* (Nashville: Cokesbury, 2004), 198-206.

47. For historical perspective on caucuses, see Kenneth E. Rowe, "How Do Caucuses Contribute to Methodism?" in Russell E. Richey, William B. Lawrence, and Dennis M. Campbell, eds., *Questions for the Twenty-first Century,* United Methodism and American Culture, vol. 4 (Nashville: Abingdon Press, 1999), 242-57.

48. Edwin H. Maynard, "The Cross and Flame: A Personal Memoir," *Methodist History,* 34:4 (July 1996), 203-13.

49. Statistical summaries are found in C. H. Jacquet, ed., *Yearbook of American and Canadian Churches, Compilation of Statistical Pages, 1916–2000.* Electronic Resource. (New York: National Council of Churches of Christ in the U.S.A., 2001). See 1969: 172, 173 for 1967 statistics and 1970: 193 for 1968 statistics.

50. *The United Methodist Newscope,* July 28, 2006. See also "Methodist ranks drop for 36th straight year," *Christian Century,* May 16, 2006, 15.

51. *General Minutes of the Annual Conferences of The United Methodist Church* (Evanston, Ill. and Nashville: General Council on Finance and Administration of The United Methodist Church). Total giving and property/asset figures have not been adjusted for inflation.

52. For an illuminating chart on United Methodist lay membership compared to the United States population, see Richey, Rowe, and Miller Schmidt, II:22.

53. *General Minutes of the Annual Conferences of The United Methodist Church* (Evanston, Ill. and Nashville: General Council on Finance and Administration).

54. *United Methodist Newscope,* October 13, 2006, 3.

55. Cf. the statistical summaries for the jurisdictions in the *General Minutes of the Annual Conferences of The United Methodist Church* to see how the membership has been shifting to the South Central and Southeastern jurisdictions. Between 1979 and 2003 the increase in membership of the southern annual conferences rose 7 percent in comparison to the annual conferences in the other three jurisdictions.

56. See for example, Douglas W. Johnson and Alan K. Waltz, *Facts and Possibilities: An Agenda for The United Methodist Church* (Nashville: Abingdon Press, 1987) and Lyle E. Schaller, *The Ice Cube Is Melting: What Is Really at Risk in United Methodism?* (Nashville: Abingdon Press, 2004). "Methodists see more no-growth churches," *Christian Century,* April 18, 2006, 16.

57. Financing ministries beyond the local church through apportionments was a practice in both the MC and the EUBC. See *DDMC*, 1964, 703 and *DEUBC*, 1967, 42-43. For a calculation on how local church dollars are spent, see http://www.umcgiving.org.

58. *BODUMC*, 1968, 24-25.

59. Cf., *BODUMC*, 2004, 29-30.

60. *Doctrines and Discipline of The Methodist Church*, 1964, 698-702.

61. *BODUMC*, 2004, 328.

62. Frank, 260.

63. Richard C. Raines, "COSMOS," in Nolan B. Harmon, ed., *The Encyclopedia of World Methodism* (Nashville: United Methodist Publishing House, 1974), I:591.

64. *BODUMC*, 2004, 662.

65. *BODUMC*, 1968, 17.

66. For example, J. Steven O'Malley, *"On the Journey Home": The History of Mission of the Evangelical United Brethren Church, 1946–1968* (New York: General Board of Global Ministries, 2003), 179 n. 3, and W. W. Reid, "World Council of Churches" in Nolan B. Harmon, ed., *The Encyclopedia of World Methodism* (Nashville: United Methodist Publishing House, 1974), II:2599.

67. Warren J. Hartman, "25 Years After Union: Was It a Good Move?" *Circuit Rider* (December 1993–January 1993): 5.

68. *BODUMC*, 1968, 441.

69. *World Methodist Council Handbook of Information 2002–2006*, Revised Edition (Lake Junaluska, N.C.: World Methodist Council, 2003), 9, 254-69.

70. "General Conference," *Encyclopedia of World Methodism*, I:955.

71. http://www.gccuic-umc.org/panmeth/mission.htm.

72. *BODUMC*, 2000, 433. For more recent information about the work of the Commission on Pan-Methodist Cooperation and Union including the proposal to change its name to Pan-Methodist Commission, see *United Methodist Newscope*, March 23, 2007, 2.

73. *BODUMC*, 2004, 342-43.

74. Robert J. Harman, *From Missions to Mission: The History of Mission of The United Methodist Church, 1968–2000* (New York: General Board of Global Ministries, 2005), 459-65.

75. For example, Nicholas Lossky et al., eds., *Dictionary of the Ecumenical Movement*, 2nd ed. (Geneva: WCC Publications, 2002), 756-60. For more extensive information on United Methodism's ecumenical conversations with Roman Catholicism, Lutheranism, Orthodox, and the Reformed, see Geoffrey Wainwright, *Methodists in Dialogue* (Nashville: Kingswood Books, 1995), and John Deschner, "United Methodism's Basic Ecumenical Policy," in Russell E. Richey, Kenneth E. Rowe, and Jean Miller Schmidt, *Perspectives* (Nashville: Kingswood Books, 1995). Kenneth E. Rowe, *United Methodist Studies: Basic Bibliographies* (Nashville: Abingdon Press, 1998), 33-42, provides an introductory bibliographic guide to books and articles about United Methodism's participation in ecumenical endeavors.

76. *BODUMC*, 1988, 116.

Chapter 4: Doctrine and Theology

1. *BODUMC*, 1972, 79.

2. *BODUMC*, 1972, 39, 70.

3. "The Principles of a Methodist Farther Explained" (1746), *The Works of John Wesley* (Bicentennial Edition), vol. 9 (Nashville: Abingdon Press, 1989), 227.

4. E-mail from Robert K. Feaster, May 4, 2006: "Schaller's books have sold well over a million total; I don't have any idea just how many. Schaller's books were always best sellers, not just with UMCs."

5. http://www.wfn.org/1999/09/msg00044.html (accessed August 30, 2006).

6. Carl Michalson, *Japanese Contributions to Christian Theology* (Philadelphia: Westminster Press, 1960), 73-99.

7. John A. T. Robinson, *Honest to God* (London: SCM Press, 1963), 118.

8. Russell E. Richey, Kenneth E. Rowe, and Jean Miller Schmidt, eds., *The Methodist Experience in America: A Sourcebook* (Nashville: Abingdon Press, 2000), II:598.

9. *BODUMC*, 1968, 36-48.

10. *BODUMC*, 2004, 27. There is a process for amending the Constitution of the United Methodist Church. It makes it possible to repeal the rule that protects the Articles of Religion, but the size of the majority required makes it all but impossible to do so in practice (*BODUMC*, 2004, 38-39).

11. Thomas A. Langford, ed., *Doctrine and Theology in The United Methodist Church* (Nashville: Kingswood Books, 1991), 20.

12. *BODUMC*, 1972, 39-82.

13. Riley B. Case, *Evangelical and Methodist: A Popular History* (Nashville: Abingdon Press, 2004), 182.

14. These account for sixteen pages in Part II of the 1972 *Discipline*, "Doctrine and Doctrinal Statements and the General Rules"; the framework of interpretation in which they are embedded covers twenty-eight pages.

15. *BODUMC*, 1972, 21-22, Restrictive Rules I, II, and V. The Constitution provides a process for amending those Restrictive Rules, but the size of the required votes makes amendment almost impossible to achieve; see *BODUMC*, 2004, 38-39.

16. *BODUMC*, 1972, 48.

17. *BODUMC*, 1972, 75.

18. *BODUMC*, 1972, 75.

19. *BODUMC*, 1972, 75.

20. Langford, 21.

21. *BODUMC*, 1972, 69.

22. *BODUMC*, 1972, 39-40.

23. *BODUMC*, 1972, 71.

24. *BODUMC*, 1972, 78.

25. *BODUMC*, 1972, 81.

26. *BODUMC*, 1972, 79.

27. *BODUMC*, 1972, 80.

28. *BODUMC*, 1972, 70.

29. *BODUMC*, 1972, 48, 40.

30. *BORUMC*, 2004, 273.

31. *BORUMC*, 2004, 273. The Articles in question are XIV, XV, XVI, XVIII, XIX, XX, and XXI. See *BODUMC*, 2004, 62 n. 4, and *BORUMC*, 2004, 271-73, "Resolution of Intent—With a View to Unity."

32. List provided by Marissa Villarreal, executive secretary for mission education, Women's Division, General Board of Global Ministries.

33. BODUMC, 1972, 78.

34. *Real* 3:3 (spring 1971): 48-71.

35. Case, 186.

36. Ibid., 183.

37. Ibid.

38. http://www.goodnewsmag.org/renewal/junaluska.htm (accessed July 25, 2006).

39. "The Junaluska Affirmation: UMC's Calvinistic Wesleyanism," *Circuit Rider*, May 1990, 4, 7.

40. Case, 245.

41. Ibid.

42. Ibid., 240.

43. Ibid.

44. Langford, 93.

45. Ibid., 94.

46. Case, 243.

47. Langford, 94-98.

48. John B. Cobb Jr., "Response to 'Bible as Decisive Authority,'" *Circuit Rider*, May 1987, 8.

49. John B. Cobb Jr., "I Say, 'Keep the Quadrilateral!'" *Circuit Rider*, May 1987, 5.

50. Case, 245.

51. Kenneth C. Kinghorn, "I Say, 'The Bible Is the Decisive Source of Authority!'" *Circuit Rider*, May 1987, 6.

52. http://www.goodnewsmag.org/renewal/houston_declaration.htm (accessed July 17, 2006).

53. Langford, 100.

54. http://www.goodnewsmag.org/renewal/houston_declaration.htm (accessed July 17, 2006).

55. Gerald H. Anderson, "The Report's Silence Presents a Serious Theological Weakness," *Circuit Rider*, February 1988, 8-9.

56. Keith J. Pohl, "General Conference—1988: In Review," *Circuit Rider*, June 1988, 16.

57. BODUMC, 1988, 40-90.

58. Langford, 106.

59. BODUMC, 1988, 47.

60. BODUMC, 1972, 39.

61. BODUMC, 1988, 51.

62. BODUMC, 1988, 60-77.

63. BODUMC, 1988, 82.

64. BODUMC, 1988, 88.

65. "To Israel with Love," *The Economist*, August 5, 2006, 28.

66. *The Works of John Wesley* (Bicentennial Edition), vol. 21 (Nashville: Abingdon Press, 1992), 401. "He now spoke as from God, what I knew God had not spoken."

67. BODUMC, 1988, 40.

68. BODUMC, 1988, 82.

69. See John Wesley's reaction to George Bell's forecast that the world would end on February 28, 1763 (*The Works of John Wesley* [Bicentennial Edition], vol. 21 [Nashville: Abingdon Press, 1992], 402, 407). Also see Wesley's comments on Revelation 12:12-15

in his *Explanatory Notes Upon the New Testament* and his chronology of the events dealt with in the book of Revelation at the end of volume 2 of his *Explanatory Notes.*

70. BODUMC, 1988, 89.

71. Case, 253.

72. Ibid., 246.

73. http://www.goodnewsmag.org/renewal/memphis_declaration.htm (accessed July 28, 2006).

74. Theodore Runyon, *The New Creation: John Wesley's Theology Today* (Nashville: Abingdon Press, 1998), 35.

75. Ibid., 219.

76. *Explanatory Notes Upon the New Testament,* Acts 10:35.

77. *The Works of John Wesley* (Bicentennial Edition), vol. 3 (Nashville: Abingdon, 1986), 296; Sermon 91, "On Charity," II.3.

78. http://confesingumc.org/v2/resources/confession.htm; also see the Indianapolis Affirmation, also see the Indianapolis Affirmation,http://confessingumc.org/indianapolis_affirmation.html (accessed July 28, 2006).

79. Pohl, 16.

80. http://www.confessingumc.org/indianapolis_affirmation.html (accessed July 10, 2006).

81. Peter J. Gomes, *The Good Book: Reading the Bible with Mind and Heart* (New York: Avon Books, 1998), 147.

82. Ibid., 162.

83. http://www.goodnewsmag.org/renewal/houston_declaration.htm (accessed July 17, 2006).

84. Case, 207.

85. Ibid., 209-10.

86. Pohl, 13.

87. Richey, Rowe, and Miller Schmidt, II:671.

88. E-mail note from Hong-ki Kim to Kenneth E. Rowe, October 9, 2006.

89. *United Methodist Newscope,* September 15, 2006, 3-4.

90. William J. Abraham, *Wesley for Armchair Theologians* (Louisville: Westminster John Knox Press, 2005), 2.

91. Runyon, 168.

92. John B. Cobb Jr., *Grace and Responsibility: A Wesleyan Theology for Today* (Nashville: Abingdon Press, 1995), 159.

93. Kenneth J. Collins, *The Scripture Way of Salvation: The Heart of John Wesley's Theology* (Nashville: Abingdon Press, 1997), 17.

94. http://www.cokesbury.com/disciple_controller.aspx?pageid=212&id=17 (accessed August 30, 2006).

95. List provided by Marisa Villarreal, Executive Secretary for Mission Education, Women's Division, General Board of Global Ministries.

96. "Sacraments: What Is Primary?" and "Feed on Him...by Faith," by Richard C. Devor, *Circuit Rider,* July/August 1987, 6.

97. "Reply to Richard" by Michael J. O'Donnell, *Circuit Rider,* July/August 1987, 7.

98. BORUMC, 2004, 857-76.

99. BORUMC, 2004, 883-931.

100. Paper read to the Phi Beta Clergy Club of the Eastern Pennsylvania Conference by David Lowes Watson, October 5, 2006.

101. BORUMC, 2004, 891.

102. *BODUMC,* 2004, 59.

103. "Religion: The God slot," *The Economist,* September 16, 2006, 38.

104. *Words That Hurt, Words That Heal: Language about God and People* (Nashville: Graded Press, 1985).

105. http://www.goodnewsmag.org/renewal/houston_declaration.htm (accessed July 17, 2006).

106. Jay W. Anderson, "God's Being and Names Must be Scriptural," *Circuit Rider,* April 1987, 5.

107. Ibid.

108. Marge Engelman, "Our Language and How Women Are Treated," *Circuit Rider,* May 1993, 4.

109. http://theologytoday.ptsem.edu/jan1991/v47-4-bookreview/3.htm (accessed August 13, 2006).

110. See Carlton R. Young, *Companion to The United Methodist Hymnal* (Nashville: Abingdon Press, 1993), 155-64.

111. Richey, Rowe, and Miller Schmidt, II:599-600.

112. http://www.gbgm-umc.org/nillconf/methesco.htm (accessed September 5, 2006).

113. *United Methodist Newscope,* February 28, 2003, 1; *Christian Century,* March 8, 2003, 12.

114. http://www.gbgm-umc.org/nillconf/methesco.htm (accessed September 5, 2006).

115. *New York Times Book Review,* Sunday, July 23, 2006, 18.

116. http://www.rickross.com/reference/fundamentalists/fund185.html (accessed August 15, 2006).

117. http://www.rickross.com/reference/fundamentalists/fund185.html (accessed August 15, 2006).

118. Langford, 21.

119. http://www.gbgm-umc.org/nillconf/methesco.htm (accessed September 5, 2006).

120. *BODUMC,* 2004, 63, 64.

121. *BORUMC,* 2004, 271-73.

122. Quoted in Richard P. Heitzenrater, *The Elusive Mr. Wesley,* vol. 1, *John Wesley His Own Biographer* (Nashville: Abingdon Press, 1984), 207.

123. Printed statement distributed at the July 23, 2006, worship service of the 19th World Methodist Conference, Kumnan Methodist Church, Seoul, Korea; "Lutherans, Catholics, Methodists in Accord," *Christian Century,* August 22, 2006.

124. *BODUMC,* 1968, 36.

Chapter 5: Worship

1. "Communion" by Third Day.

2. *BODUMC,* 1968, 20; 2004, 26.

3. *BODUMC,* 1968, 439.

4. *BODUMC,* 1988, 512.

5. *The United Methodist Hymnal* (Nashville: United Methodist Publishing House, 1989), 2.

6. Ibid., 3-31.

7. Ibid., 32-54.

8. *BODUMC*, 1992, 500.

9. *BODUMC*, 1996, 475. In 1973, the United Methodist Publishing House issued *Himnario Metodista*, a Spanish-language hymnal based on an earlier hymnal of the Rio Grande Annual Conference.

10. This bilingual Korean-English hymnal was approved by the 2000 General Conference and published the next year by the United Methodist Publishing House.

11. *BODUMC*, 2000, 505.

12. *BODUMC*, 2004, 528.

13. Carlton R. Young, *Companion to the United Methodist Hymnal* (Nashville: Abingdon Press, 1993), 135-37.

14. Ibid., 136.

15. *BODUMC*, 1984, 99.

16. "Therefore it was called Babel, because there the Lord confused the language of all the earth" (Genesis 11:9). The Hebrew *balal* means "to confuse."

17. Exodus 3:14. Other possible ways to translate the Hebrew are "I AM WHO I AM" and "I AM WHAT I AM."

18. John A. T. Robinson, *Honest to God* (London: SCM Press, 1963), 13.

19. Ibid., 45.

20. Methodist Article of Religion I—Of Faith in the Holy Trinity—makes clear that God is *without* gender, *above* gender, by asserting that God is "without body or parts" (*BODUMC*, 2004, 59).

21. Westminster Press (Philadelphia) published Years A, B, and C of the *Inclusive Language Lectionary* in 1983, 1984, and 1985.

22. Burton H. Throckmorton Jr., "Why the Inclusive Language Lectionary?" *Christian Century*, August 1-8, 1984, 742.

23. "An Inclusive Language Lectionary (1983–85), accessed at http://www.bible-researcher.com/ill.html (accessed February 18, 2007).

24. Throckmorton.

25. Young, 123-25.

26. *BORUMC*, 1984, 241-42.

27. Reply from United Methodist Information Service, December 12, 2006.

28. *Words That Hurt, Words That Heal: Language about God and People* (Nashville: Graded Press, 1985); revised edition, 1990.

29. Young, 126-27.

30. Riley B. Case, *Evangelical and Methodist: A Popular History* (Nashville: Abingdon Press, 2004), 229.

31. Young, 127.

32. Ibid., 159-64.

33. Russell E. Richey, Kenneth E. Rowe, and Jean Miller Schmidt, eds., *The Methodist Experience in America* (Nashville: Abingdon Press, 2000), II:653.

34. Young, 138.

35. *Hymnal*, 1989, 240.

36. Ibid., 698.

37. Ibid., 224.

38. Richey, Rowe, and Miller Schmidt, II:654.

39. Young, 141; *Hymnal*, 1989, 105. This imagery is at least as old as the "Hymn on the Nativity, Number 4" written by one of John Wesley's favorite early-church writers,

Ephrem of Syria (died 373). Ephrem speaks of Jesus as having a womb in which "dwells all creation," and as "the Living Breast of living breath" (Robert Atwan, George Dardess, and Peggy Rosenthal, eds., *Divine Inspiration: The Life of Jesus in World Poetry* [New York: Oxford University Press, 1998], 21).

40. Young, 142.

41. Keith J. Pohl, "General Conference—1988: In Review," *Circuit Rider*, June 1988, 15.

42. *Hymnal*, 1989, 261.

43. Young, 171; Pohl, 15.

44. The new hymnal of the Evangelical Lutheran Church suggests this alternative for "Father, Son, and Holy Spirit" (*United Methodist Newscope*, August 26, 2005, 4).

45. *BODUMC*, 1988, 42.

46. *Hymnal*, 1989, 37.

47. *BODUMC*, 1988, 240; *Book of Worship*, 1992, 693, 696; "As these services [ordinations, and so forth] are acts of the whole Church, text and rubrics are to be used as approved by the General Conference" (*BODUMC*, 2004, 299).

48. *Book of Worship*, 1992, 563.

49. Resolution on "Biblical Language," BORUMC, 1988, 596.

50. "Re-re-imagining in Minnesota—feminist religious conference," *Christian Century*, December 20, 1995.

51. "Paganism at the Re-Imagining Conference in Minneapolis (1993)," editorial, *Brethren Revival Fellowship Witness* 29, no. 3 (May/June 1994).

52. Case, 255-56.

53. Richey, Rowe, and Miller Schmidt, II:673.

54. BORUMC, 2000, 817; BORUMC, 2004, 876.

55. *BODUMC*, 2004, 328.

56. *BODUMC*, 2004, 332.

57. *Circuit Rider*, December 1996/January 1997, 4, 8, 5, 10, 9.

58. Special report: Peter Drucker—"Trusting the teacher in the grey-flannel suit," *The Economist*, November 19, 2005, 72.

59. "Jesus, CEO: America's most successful churches are modeling themselves on businesses," *The Economist*, December 24, 2005, 41.

60. Thomas G. Long, *Beyond the Worship Wars: Building Vital and Faithful Worship* (Herndon, Va.: The Alban Institute, 2001), 7.

61. Mark Chaves, "Supersized: Analyzing the trend toward larger churches," *Christian Century*, November 28, 2006, 20-25.

62. "Openness to Change Plays Role in Church Growth," *United Methodist Newscope*, January 26, 2007, 1.

63. Bruce Wilkinson, *The Prayer of Jabez: Breaking Through to the Blessed Life* (Sisters, Oreg.: Multnomah Publishers, 2005; first published in 2000).

64. 1 Chronicles 4:10 NRSV.

65. http://www.lighthousetrailresearch.com/prayerofjabez.htm (accessed August 16, 2006).

66. William H. Willimon, "It's Hard to Be Seeker-Sensitive When You Work for Jesus," *Circuit Rider*, September/October 2003, 4-5.

67. Baby Boomers are persons born in 1946 and the following years, through 1964.

68. *Hymnal*, 1989, 3-5.

69. Long, 4.

70. The first Christians "devoted themselves to the apostles' teaching and fellowship, to the breaking of bread and the prayers" (Acts 2:42).

71. Justin Martyr, *First Apology* (about 155); James F. White, *Documents of Christian Worship* (Louisville, Ky.: Westminster John Knox Press, 1992), 185.

72. White, 185.

73. Ibid., 186-87.

74. *Hymnal*, 1989, 1-54.

75. *Book of Worship*, 1992, 13-114.

76. "A Service of Christian Marriage, with Introduction, Commentary and Additional Resources" (principal drafters, M. Lawrence Snow and Robert E. Scoggin), 1979; "A Service of Death and Resurrection: The Ministry of the Church at Death" (principal drafter, Paul W. Hoon), 1979.

77. *Hymnal*, 1989, 2-5. See Acts 2:42. Justin Martyr, *First Apology* (about 155): "And on the day called Sunday there is a meeting in one place of those who live in cities or the country, and the memoirs of the apostles or the writings of the prophets are read as long as time permits. When the reader has finished, the president in a discourse urges and invites [us] to the imitation of these noble things. Then we all stand up together and offer prayers. And, ... when we have finished the prayer, bread is brought, and wine and water, and the president similarly sends up prayers and thanksgivings to the best of his ability, and the congregation assents, saying the Amen; the distribution, and reception of the consecrated [elements] by each one, takes place and they are sent to the absent by the deacons" (White, 185-86).

78. See "An Order of Sunday Worship Using the Basic Pattern" (*Hymnal*, 1989, 3-5).

79. The subdivisions are: Gathering, Greeting and Hymn, and Opening Prayer and Praise.

80. Luke 24:29.

81. The subheads under "Proclamation and Response" are: Prayer for Illumination; Scripture; Sermon; Response to the Word; Concerns and Prayers; Confession, Pardon, and Peace; and Offering.

82. Revised Common Lectionary, *Book of Worship*, 1992, 227-37.

83. This division allows for celebrating Holy Communion or omitting it.

84. Luke 24:30-31.

85. The subdivisions are "Hymn or Song and Dismissal with Blessing" and "Going Forth."

86. Luke 24:33, 35.

87. John Wesley's letter to "Dr. Coke, Mr. Asbury, and our Brethren in North-America," September 10, 1784; *The Sunday Service of the Methodists in North America* (facsimile, Nashville: United Methodist Publishing House, 1992), iii.

88. *Sunday Service*, ii.

89. Robert Faggen, ed., *The Notebooks of Robert Frost* (Cambridge: Harvard University Press, 2006), 97.

90. BORUMC, 2004, 857-76.

91. BORUMC, 2004, 883-931.

92. *Hymnal*, 1989, 36.

93. Ibid., 37.

94. Ibid., 10.

95. Ibid., 11.

96. Ibid., 11.

97. Karen B. Westerfield Tucker, *American Methodist Worship* (New York: Oxford University Press, 2001), 110.

98. http://www.elca.org/ecumenical/ecumenicaldislogue/unitedmethodist/index.html (accessed February 22, 2007).

99. "Baptism, Eucharist, and Ministry, Responses and Reception" (*BORUMC*, 1984, 283).

100. Adrian Hastings, ed., *The Oxford Companion to Christian Thought* (New York: Oxford University Press, 2000), 60.

101. Gayle C. Felton, *This Gift of Water: The Practice and Theology of Baptism among Methodists in America* (Nashville: Abingdon Press, 1993).

102. Gayle Carlton Felton, "The Committee Points the Way to the Richness and Understanding of Making Christians," *Circuit Rider*, February 1992, 9.

103. *BORUMC*, 1996, 716-35.

104. *BORUMC*, 1996, 722.

105. *BORUMC*, 1992, 22.

106. *BORUMC*, 2004, 22.

107. See "Seminary Professor James White Introduces Revised Rite for Holy Communion" in Richey, Rowe, and Miller Schmidt, II:627-30.

108. *Oxford Companion to Christian Thought*, 214.

109. "Now That We Have an Official Statement [*This Holy Mystery: A United Methodist Understanding of Holy Communion*], So What?"—a presentation made by Gayle Carlton Felton at a conference titled "This Holy Mystery: Teaching the Sacrament—Improving Our Practice," April 26-28, 2005, in Nashville, Tennessee.

110. "The Great Thanksgiving," A Service of Word and Table I, *Hymnal*, 1989, 10.

111. Sermon 26, "Sermon on the Mount, VI," III.11, *The Works of John Wesley* (Bicentennial Edition), vol. 1 (Nashville: Abingdon Press, 1984), 584-85.

112. John and Charles Wesley, *Hymns on the Lord's Supper*, facsimile of the 1745 Bristol edition (Madison: Charles Wesley Society, 1995), 39, Hymn LIV.

113. Charles Wesley used "?" not "!" after this line in his hymn; Hymn LVII, *Hymns on the Lord's Supper*, 41.

114. *Hymnal*, 1989, 627.

115. See note no. 114.

116. Daniel B. Stevick, *Altar's Fire* (Peterborough, U.K.: Epworth Press, 2004).

117. *BORUMC*, 1996, 714; *BORUMC*, 2004, 920.

118. All Christians used wine for the Lord's Supper until the late nineteenth century, when Thomas Welch pasteurized grape juice employing the milk-pasteurization process. When this happened, Methodists, Evangelicals, and United Brethren began to substitute grape juice for wine, a practice that soon was mandated. This mandate was omitted, however, when the reshaped rite was approved, and a few United Methodists began to use wine.

119. *BORUMC*, 2004, 884-931.

120. Gayle Carlton Felton, *This Holy Mystery: A United Methodist Understanding of Holy Communion* (Nashville: Discipleship Resources, 2005).

121. Carolyn Tanner, *This Holy Mystery: A United Methodist Understanding of Holy Communion—A Study Guide for Children and Youth* (Akron, Ohio: OSL Publications, 2006).

122. "Lutherans Approve Interim Agreement with UMs," *United Methodist Newscope*, August 19, 2005, 3.

123. "Lutheran Body Wants Eucharist Shared with UMs," *United Methodist Newscope*, April 29, 2005, 3.

124. "ELCA adopts accord with Methodists, stance on Israel, new hymnal," *Christian Century*, September 6, 2005, 13.

125. *United Methodist Newscope*, October 6, 2006, 3.

126. Ibid., February 16, 2007, 3.

127. "Proposal Offered to Start Process for Hymnal Revision," *United Methodist Newscope*, September 7, 2007, 3.

Chapter 6: Ministry

1. *BODUMC*, 2004, 89.

2. Richard P. Heitzenrater, "A Critical Analysis of the Ministry Studies Since 1948," in Russell E. Richey, Kenneth E. Rowe, and Jean Miller Schmidt, eds., *Perspectives on American Methodism: Interpretive Essays* (Nashville: Abingdon Press, 1993), 431-47. An important Methodist historical survey prior to the union is Gerald O. McCullough, ed., *The Ministry in the Methodist Heritage* (Nashville: Board of Education, The Methodist Church, 1960).

3. *Report to the Uniting Conference of The United Methodist Church. The Committee to Study the Ministry* (Dallas, 1968), 10.

4. *BODUMC*, 1968, 106-7.

5. *BODUMC*, 1976, 107. See also, Kenneth E. Rowe, "All Are Called: Thoughts on 'The Ministry of All Christians' in the United Methodist Tradition," unpublished paper prepared for United Methodist polity course, Princeton Theological Seminary, Spring 2007.

6. *BODUMC*, 2000, 87-94, which provides a more detailed theological description of the ministry to which all Christians are called and obligated. This section remains in the same place in *BODUMC*, 2004, 87-94.

7. *BODUMC*, 1976, 30.

8. *General Minutes of the Annual Conferences of The United Methodist Church*, 1980, 1102; 2000, 1156.

9. See the basic history of the deaconess movement in Mary Agnes Dougherty, *My Calling to Fulfill: Deaconesses in The United Methodist Tradition* (New York: Women's Division, General Board of Global Ministries, 1997). For provisions for the office of lay missioner, see *BODUMC*, 2004, 563.

10. *BODUMC*, 1992, 195.

11. *BODUMC*, 2004, 352.

12. For example, see the most recent provisions in *BODUMC*, 2004, 281-83. A comparison of the *General Minutes of the Annual Conferences of The United Methodist Church* (Evanston, Ill.: General Council on Finance and Administration, 1993, 1347-53, and Nashville: 2004, 1243-45) illustrates the steep decline in the numbers of diaconal ministers.

13. *BODUMC*, 1968, 377.

14. *DDMC*, 1964, 137-38.

15. *BODUMC*, 1980, 167.

16. *BODUMC*, 1992, 184-88.

17. *BODUMC*, 2004, 192.

18. *BODUMC*, 2004, 192-93.

19. News release, "Competition Under Way for General Conference Laity Address," United Methodist News Service, February 9, 1999.

20. *DDMC*, 1964, 141-45.

21. *DEUBC*, 1967, 87.

22. *BODUMC*, 1968, 123.

23. *BODUMC*, 1976, 170-71.

24. *BODUMC*, 1980, 192, 289-90. For a concise discussion of the role of local pastors, see Thomas Edward Frank, *Polity, Practice, and the Mission of The United Methodist Church* (Nashville: Abingdon Press, 2006), 206-10.

25. *BODUMC*, 1996, 309.

26. *BODUMC*, 1980, 309.

27. *Report to the Uniting Conference The United Methodist Church. The Committee to Study the Ministry* (Dallas, 1968), 14-15.

28. *The Study of Ministry, 1960–1964* (Nashville: Board of Education, 1964).

29. Heitzenrater, 434-35.

30. Progress on the work of the Commission is reported in *The United Methodist Newscope*, May 5, 2006, 18.

31. "Ordained and Diaconal Ministries," *DCA Advance Edition* (Nashville, 1996), I:969-81.

32. See *BODUMC*, 1980, 107-8.

33. "Ordained and Diaconal Ministries," 975.

34. Ibid., 976.

35. Ibid.

36. Ibid., 977-79.

37. Ibid., 979-80.

38. News Release, United Methodist News Service, April 25, 1996.

39. *General Minutes of the Annual Conferences of The United Methodist Church* (Evanston, Ill.: General Council on Finance and Administration, 1969), 29.

40. Statistics supplied by the General Council on Finance and Administration.

41. See Patricia J. Thompson, *Courageous Past—Bold Future—The Journey toward Full Clergy Rights for Women in The United Methodist Church* (Nashville: General Board of Higher Education and Ministry, 2006). See also, Rosemary S. Keller, "Women and the Nation of Ministry in the United Methodist Tradition," *Methodist History*, XXII, no. 2 (January 1984): 99-114.

42. Donald K. Gorrell, ed., *Woman's Rightful Place* (Dayton, Ohio: United Theological Seminary, 1980), 32. Thompson, 64-67.

43. *Circuit Rider*, March/April 2006, 4-7. See also the important and revealing report of the Lewis Center for Church Leadership, http://www.churchleadership.com/research/um_clergy_age_trends.htm.

44. Episcopacy in Methodism and United Methodism is described historically with commentary and proposals for change by Russell E. Richey and Thomas Edward Frank, *Episcopacy in the Methodist Tradtion: Perspectives and Proposals* (Nashville: Abingdon Press, 2004).

45. *DEUBC*, 1967, 101-2; *DDMC*, 1964, 24,

46. *DDMC*, 1964, 182-83, 196.

47. *DEUBC*, 1967, 103-4.

48. *DDMC*, 1964, 24-25.

49. James K. Mathews and William B. Oden, eds., *Vision and Supervision: A Sourcebook of Significant Documents of the Council of Bishops of The United Methodist Church, 1968–2002* (Nashville: Abingdon Press, 2003) provides an invaluable collection of documents and information regarding the life of the Council.

50. See the foundation document produced by the Council of Bishops, *Vital Congregations—Faithful Disciples* (Nashville: Graded Press, 1990).

51. For full or partial texts of these documents, see Mathews and Oden, 55-100.

52. Ibid., 243-66.

53. Ibid., 17. This action was permitted by the BODUMC, 1968, 141.

54. BODUMC, 1996, 259.

55. *The 2005 United Methodist Directory & Index of Resources* (Nashville: Cokesbury, 2005), 2.

56. Ibid.

57. *DDMC*, 1964, 159-62, 176.

58. *DEUBC*, 1964, 94-95.

59. *BODUMC*, 1968, 130, 143.

60. *BODUMC*, 1992, 282.

61. This statistic was supplied by the Division of Ordained Ministry, General Board of Higher Education and Ministry.

62. *DEUBC*, 1967, 52. Cf. *DDMC*, 1964, 432.

63. *DEUBC*, 1967, 52.

64. For example, *DDMC*, 1964, 177.

65. *BODUMC*, 1968, 131.

66. *BODUMC*, 1980, 253-55.

67. Some of these issues are discussed in more detail in Thomas Edward Frank, *Polity, Practice, and the Mission of The United Methodist Church* (Nashville: Abingdon Press, 2006), 218-28, and in *Circuit Rider*, May/June 2005, the whole issue of which is devoted to the itinerancy.

68. *DDMC*, 1964, 176.

69. *BODUMC*, 1980, 252.

70. *BODUMC*, 2004, 307. See also the important manual on cross-racial and cross-cultural ministry with practical suggestions for implementation, Ernest S. Lyght, Glory E. Dharmaraj, and Jacob S. Dharmaraj, *Many Faces One Church: A Manual for Cross-Racial and Cross-Cultural Ministry* (Nashville: Abingdon Press, 2006).

71. *BODUMC*, 1972, 165-66.

72. *BODUMC*, 1976, 207-8.

73. *BODUMC*, 1996, 222-27.

74. A list of the current schools, colleges, universities, and seminaries is found in the annual *United Methodist Directory & Index of Resources* (Nashville: Cokesbury).

75. "Report of the Commission to Study the Ministry of The United Methodist Church," *General Conference Journal*, 1972, 1711-31.

76. Ibid., 1723.

77. Ibid., 1725-29.

78. See the following website for more information, http://public.gbhem.org/iamscu/schools.asp.

79. See *BODUMC*, 1968, 132.

80. "Report of the Commission to Study the Ministry of The United Methodist Church," 1730.

81. For example, see BODUMC, 2004, 255-56.

Chapter 7: Mission

1. Thomas Jackson, ed., *The Works of John Wesley*, 3rd edition (Grand Rapids, Mich.: Baker Book House, 1996), 8:299.

2. Quoted in Russell E. Richey, Kenneth E. Rowe, and Jean Miller Schmidt, eds., *The Methodist Experience in America: A Sourcebook* (Nashville: Abingdon Press, 2000), 82.

3. For example, Methodist Episcopal Church mission work, 1769 to 1939, was thoroughly described in four volumes. See Wade Crawford Barclay, *History of Methodist Missions*, 3 vols. (New York: Board of Missions of the Methodist Church, 1949–57) and J. Tremayne Copplestone, *History of Methodist Missions*, vol. 4 (New York: Board of Global Ministries of the United Methodist Church, 1973).

4. J. Steven O'Malley, *"On the Journey Home": The History of Mission of the Evangelical United Brethren Church, 1946–1968* (New York: General Board of Global Ministries, The United Methodist Church, 2003); Ruth A. Daugherty, *The Missionary Spirit: The History of Mission of the Methodist Protestant Church, 1830–1939* (New York: General Board of Global Ministries, The United Methodist Church, 2004); Robert W. Sledge, *"Five Dollars and Myself": The History of Mission of the Methodist Episcopal Church, South, 1845–1939* (New York: General Board of Global Ministries, The United Methodist Church, 2005); Linda Gesling, *Mirror and Beacon: The History of Mission of The Methodist Church, 1939–1968* (New York: General Board of Global Ministries, The United Methodist Church, 2005); Robert J. Harman, *From Missions to Mission: The History of Mission of The United Methodist Church, 1968 2000* (New York: General Board of Global Ministries, The United Methodist Church, 2005); and Charles E. Cole, ed., *Initiatives for Mission, 1980–2002* (New York: General Board of Global Ministries, The United Methodist Church, 2003).

5. *DEUBC*, 1963, 260.

6. *DDMC*, 1964, 341.

7. *BODUMC*, 1968, 363.

8. *BODUMC*, 1972, 234.

9. *Daily Christian Advocate*, Advance Edition, E 19-22, C 15-23.

10. The recommended study document is *Grace Upon Grace: The Mission Statement of The United Methodist Church* (Nashville: Graded Press, 1990).

11. *BODUMC*, 1996, 114.

12. See his commentary on the mission statement in "Proclaiming Salvation—Making Disciples," in James K. Mathews and William B. Oden, eds., *Vision and Supervision: A Sourcebook of Significant Documents of the Council of Bishops of The United Methodist Church, 1968–2002* (Nashville: Abingdon Press, 2003), 344-60.

13. *BODUMC*, 1996, 309.

14. *BODUMC*, 1996, 397.

15. O'Malley, 151-70.

16. Ibid., 35-150.

17. Ibid., 181.

18. For statistics on missionaries outside the United States, and even a listing of their names, see Gesling, 324-404.

19. *DDMC*, 1964, 247-51.

20. *BODUMC*, 1972, 355-56.

21. "Mission Executive Tracey Jones Looks to the Future," Richey, Rowe, and Miller Schmidt, 618-19.

22. For example, see "Methodist Delegate Arlo Ayres Brown Supports Findings of Ecumenical Laymen's Foreign Missions Inquiry," in Richey, Rowe, and Schmidt, 529-31, in which Brown in 1932 called for a new missionary philosophy that would result in indigenous, self-supporting churches.

23. "Bishop Muzorewa Cites Missionary Mistakes Made in Africa," in Richey, Rowe, and Miller Schmidt, 641-42

24. Barclay, III:170-71.

25. W. Richey Hogg, "The Missions of American Methodism," in Emory Stevens Bucke, ed., *The History of American Methodism* (Nashville: Abingdon Press, 1964), III:111.

26. Too little has been done to record the histories of the central conferences of United Methodism that exist in Africa, Europe, and the Philippines. Some information on Europe is found in Patrick Ph. Streiff, *Methodism in Europe: 19th and 20th Century* (Tallinn, Estonia: Baltic Methodist Theological Seminary, 2003).

27. *BODUMC*, 2004, 328.

28. Mansfield Hurtig, "Russia," in Nolan B. Harmon, ed., *The Encyclopedia of World Methodism* (Nashville: The United Methodist Publishing House, 1974), II:2057-58.

29. For detailed information on the establishment of United Methodist mission work in Russia, see Harman, 299-323.

30. Streiff, 245.

31. Harman, 316.

32. Ibid., 331.

33. *BODUMC*, 1980, 366.

34. Harman, 246-58.

35. *BODUMC*, 1992, 401.

36. Harman, 260-74. For more information on the shalom ministry, see "Shalom Zones Celebrated," United Methodist Daily News release #047, April 24, 1996.

37. "Shalom Zones Celebrated," United Methodist News Service Release #047, April 24, 1996.

38. Mathews and Oden, 82-100.

39. Cole, 66. Statistics on the number of missionaries supported by the denomination are published in the annual reports of the General Board of Global Ministries.

40. Harman, 118.

41. *BODUMC*, 1980, 462.

42. *BODUMC*, 1996, 506-7.

43. Harman, 122.

44. For a brief description of the origins and early development of these mission courses, see "Missionary Education," in *The Methodist Woman*, February 1959, 34.

45. Rupert E. Davies, ed., *The Methodist Societies: History, Nature, and Design*. The Works of John Wesley, vol. 9 (Nashville: Abingdon Press, 1989), 72.

46. *DEUBC*, 1967, 252.

47. *DEUBC*, 1967, 89.

48. *DEUBC*, 197, 252-58.

49. *DDMC*, 1964, 442.

50. *BODUMC*, 1968, 321.

51. *BODUMC*, 1968, 322, 327, 330, 96.

52. *BODUMC*, 1972, 332-37.

53. *BODUMC*, 2004, 526.

54. Mathews and Oden, 253-54.

55. Ibid., 74. See the study materials published for local churches, *Vital Congregations, Faithful Disciples: Vision for the Church, Foundation Document, the Council of Bishops of The United Methodist Church* (Nashville: Graded Press, 1990).

56. *DEUB*, 1963, 345.

57. *DDMC*, 1964, 471.

58. *BODUMC*, 1968, 385-86.

59. *BODUMC*, 1972, 374.

60. "$16 M ends United Methodist role in Pacific Homes," United Methodist News Service, March 31, 1999, and "United Methodists' Pacific Homes saga ends on an up note," United Methodist News Service, September 10, 1999. See also Harman, 190-91.

61. *BODUMC*, 2004, 397, 572.

62. *BODUMC*, 2004, 184.

63. *BODUMC*, 2004, 503-5. The fiftieth anniversary of the Advance program was celebrated in 1998. In the years since its founding the Advance has received more than 3 million gifts totaling more than $1.5 billion.

64. *United Methodist Newscope*, July 28, 2006, 3.

65. See, for example, the initiative on Restorative Justice and Mercy Ministries adopted by the 1996 General Conference, *Daily Christian Advocate*, April 27, 1996, 741.

66. *The 2005 United Methodist Directory & Index of Resources* (Nashville: Cokesbury, 2005), 210-20.

67. Merrimon Cuninggim, *Uneasy Partners: The College and the Church* (Nashville: Abingdon Press, 1994) and George M. Marsden, *The Soul of the American University: From Protestant Establishment to Established Nonbelief* (New York: Oxford University Press, 1994), and Douglas Sloan, *Faith and Knowledge: Mainline Protestantism and American Higher Education* (Louisville, Ky.: Westminster John Knox Press, 1994).

68. For more information, see the university's website: http://www.africau.edu.

69. Riley B. Case, *Evangelical and Methodist: A Popular History* (Nashville: Abingdon Press, 2004), 102.

70. Ibid.

71. Ibid., 104.

72. Harman, 90-91.

73. Case, 109-15.

74. See "Mission Statement" on website: http://www.ird-renew.org/site.

75. Case, 117; Harman, 155-56, 236.

76. Case, 127. See the comments regarding the actions of the 1984 General Conference in Harman, 170 n. 15.

77. *Good News*, March/April 1984, 54-62.

78. See his comments, "The Impact of an Independent Missions Agency" in Harman, 178-83.

79. Harman, 183-87.

80. O'Malley, 181.

81. Ibid.

82. *BODEUBC,* 1963, 264, 324.

83. *DDMC,* 1964, 482-84.

84. *BODUMC,* 1980, 566-68.

85. Cf. *BODUMC,* 1980, 566, and *BODUMC,* 2004, 649.

86. "Independent Puerto Rican Church Elects First Bishop," News release, United Methodist News Service, November 17, 1992.

87. Jose Gamboa, *Methodism in the Philippines: A Century of Faith and Vision* (Manila: Phippines Central Conference, The United Methodist Church, 2003).

88. Harman, 221.

89. *Daily Christian Advocate,* Advance Edition, 1988, C 16.

Chapter 8: Social Engagement

1. An amendment to the Constitution, an unusually difficult one to adopt, is required to change the Articles of Religion and the Confession of Faith; see *BODUMC,* 2004, 38-39.

2. This point is developed fully by Darryl W. Stephens, "A Witness of Words: The United Methodist Social Principles as Moral Discourse and Institutional Practice" (Ph.D. dissertation, Emory University, 2006), 140-45.

3. *BODUMC,* 1968, 53-66.

4. Earl D. C. Brewer, *Continuation or Transformation? The Involvement of United Methodism in Social Movements and Issues* (Nashville: Abingdon Press, 1982), 34.

5. The Federal Council of Churches was founded in 1908.

6. Frederick A. Norwood, *The Story of American Methodism* (Nashville: Abingdon Press, 1974), 354; Charles Yrigoyen Jr. and Susan E. Warrick, eds., *Historical Dictionary of Methodism* (Lanham: Scarecrow Press, 2005), 281-82.

7. *BODUMC,* 1968, 59. This is the statement in the EUB Basic Beliefs: "The Church protests against all acts and practices of discrimination which are based upon racial, national, creedal or social differences" (*BODUMC,* 1968, 65).

8. Letters of John Wesley to the Earl of Dartmouth, June 14, August 23, and December 24, 1775 (John Telford, ed., *The Letters of John Wesley,* vol. 6 [London: Epworth Press, 1960], 155-60, 175-76, 198-99).

9. John Wesley's Journal, October 1, 1759 (*The Works of John Wesley* [Bicentennial Edition], vol. 21 [Nashville: Abingdon Press, 1992], 231); also see Wesley's letter to the editor of *Lloyd's Evening Post,* October 20, 1759 (John Telford, ed., *The Letters of John Wesley,* vol. 4 [London: Epworth Press, 1960], 73-74); compare Samuel Johnson's "Introduction to Proceedings of the Committee on French Prisoners," 1760 (Samuel Johnson, *Political Writings* [New Haven: Yale University Press, 1977], 285-89).

10. V. H. H. Green, *John Wesley* (Lanham: University Press of America, 1987), 32; Vivian Green, *The Commonwealth of Lincoln College, 1427–1977* (Oxford: Oxford University Press, 1979), 341-42; V. H. H. Green, *A History of Oxford University* (London: B. T. Batsford, 1974), 126.

11. John Wesley, "Thoughts upon Slavery" (1774), *The Works of John Wesley* (Jackson Edition), vol. 11 (Grand Rapids, Mich.: Zondervan, n.d., reprint of 1872 London edition), 79.

12. Arthur M. Schlesinger Jr., "Folly's Antidote," *New York Times*, January 1, 2007.

13. The Eighteenth Amendment to the United States Constitution, which was ratified in 1919, prohibited the manufacture, sale, import, or export of liquor in the United States. It was repealed in 1933.

14. Pete Hamill, "Raging Thirst," a review of *Dry Manhattan: Prohibition in New York City* by Michael A. Lerner, *New York Times Book Review*, March 11, 2007, 9.

15. John A. T. Robinson, *Honest to God* (London: SCM Press, 1963), 118.

16. John G. McEllhenney, *Cutting the Monkey Rope* (Valley Forge: Judson Press, 1973), 91.

17. Ibid.

18. *BODUMC*, 1972, 87.

19. *BODUMC*, 1972, 94.

20. *BODUMC*, 1972, 96; also war is declared "incompatible with the gospel and spirit of Christ," 95.

21. *BODUMC*, 1972, 95.

22. *BODUMC*, 1972, 84.

23. *BODUMC*, 1972, 86-87.

24. See *Becoming Justice Blackmun: Harry Blackmun's Supreme Court Journey* by Linda Greenhouse (New York: Times Books/Henry Holt & Company, 2005).

25. Quoted by Jeffrey Rosen in "A Pivotal Justice Less Than Supremely Confident," a review of *Becoming Justice Blackmun* by Linda Greenhouse, *New York Times*, May 6, 2005.

26. California's 1969 law was the first.

27. *BODUMC*, 1972, 85-86.

28. *BORUMC*, 1968, 49-50.

29. "Professional Associations' statements about Homosexuality," accessed at http://religioustolerance.org/hom_prof.htm (accessed March 19, 2007).

30. Quoted in James Waller, "'Half-Queer Themselves': San Francisco's Council on Religion and the Homosexual," a paper presented to the annual meeting of the Mid-Atlantic Region of the American Academy of Religion in Baltimore, Maryland, March, 1996.

31. Russell E. Richey, Kenneth E. Rowe, and Jean Miller Schmidt, *The Methodist Experience in America: A Sourcebook* (Nashville: Abingdon Press, 2000), II:622.

32. *BODUMC*, 1972, 86.

33. *BODUMC*, 1976, 98.

34. *BODUMC*, 1976, 98.

35. *BODUMC*, 1976, 99.

36. Philip Jenkins, *Decade of Nightmares: The End of the Sixties and the Making of Eighties America* (New York: Oxford University Press, 2006), 85.

37. The Equal Rights Amendment died in 1982, having failed to be ratified by the thirty-eight states necessary for passage.

38. Jenkins, 120.

39. "Prime responsibility of the [Board of Church and Society] is to implement the Social Creed" (*BODUMC*, 1972, 307; see also 307-8). This is the 2004 statement: "The prime responsibility of the [General Board of Church and Society] is to seek the imple-

mentation of the Social Principles and other policy statements of the General Conference on Christian social concerns.... The board shall analyze long-range social trends and their underlying ethical values. It shall explore systemic strategies for social change and alternative futures. It shall speak its convictions, interpretations, and concerns to the Church and to the world" (*BODUMC*, 2004, 512-13).

40. *BODUMC*, 2004, 317.

41. *BODUMC*, 2004, 315.

42. This information was provided by Marisa Villarreal, executive secretary for mission education, Women's Division, General Board of Global Ministries.

43. Riley B. Case, *Evangelical and Methodist: A Popular History* (Nashville: Abingdon, 2004), 209.

44. "A Brief History of Affirmation," accessed at http://www.umaffirm.org/afhistory.html (accessed November 28, 2006).

45. Ibid.

46. "Since the practice of homosexuality is incompatible with Christian teaching, self-avowed practicing homosexuals are not to be accepted as candidates, ordained as ministers, or appointed to serve in The United Methodist Church" (*BODUMC*, 1984, 189).

47. This became the Reconciling Ministries Network in 2000.

48. "A Brief History of Affirmation."

49. Methodist Federation for Social Action website: accessed at http://www.mfsa.org/whoweare (accessed November 28, 2006).

50. Methodist Federation for Social Action website, http://www.mfsaweb.org/whoweare.

51. *BODUMC*, 2004, 305.

52. Richey, Rowe, and Miller Schmidt, II:655-56.

53. Tom McAnally, "Bishops renew, advance their initiative on children, poverty," May 4, 2001; accessed at http://archives.umc.org/umns/news_archive 2001 (accessed November 29, 2006).

54. Letter of Bishop Sharon A. Brown Christopher to President George W. Bush, February 6, 2003; accessed at http://search.umc.org (accessed November 15, 2006).

55. James Mathews and William Oden, *Vision and Supervision* (Nashville: Abingdon Press), 2003.

56. *BODUMC*, 2004, 328.

57. *BODUMC*, 2004, 30; also see 331.

58. Press Release, United Methodist Church in Austria, Fifth International Consultation; accessed at http://www.emk.at/aktuell/InformationKonsultation.html (accessed July 26, 2006).

59. Darryl W. Stephens, unpublished manuscript, "European Adaptations of the Social Principles."

60. Ibid.

61. The Africa Central Conference is composed of annual conferences in Angola, Botswana, Burundi, Kenya, Malawi, Mozambique, Namibia, Rwanda, South Africa, Sudan, Uganda, Zambia, and Zimbabwe (*BODUMC*, 2004, 328).

62. Darryl W. Stephens, "Face of Unity or Mask over Difference? The Social Principles in the Central Conferences of The United Methodist Church," *Thinking About Religion*, vol. 5 (2005); accessed at http://organizations.uncfsu.edu/ncrsa/journal/v05/stephens_face.htm (accessed August 3, 2006).

63. Ibid.

64. Paper prepared by Darryl Stephens for John G. McEllhenney, September 9, 2006.

65. Stephens, "Face of Unity."

66. Some African nations "impose stiffer penalties for homosexual acts than for rape and murder" (Sharon LaFraniere, "South African Parliament Approves Same-Sex Marriages," *New York Times*, November 15, 2006).

67. Stephens, "A Witness of Words: The United Methodist Social Principles as Moral Discourse and Institutional Practice," 143. This statement was in Petition 30260 submitted by the Africa Central Conference to the 2000 General Conference; it was voided by the Committee on Reference.

68. *BODUMC*, 2004, 100.

69. Stephens, "Face of Unity."

70. *BODUMC*, 1980, 86.

71. *BODUMC*, 1980, 93.

72. *BODUMC*, 1980, 97.

73. *BODUMC*, 1980, 103.

74. *BODUMC*, 1984, 99.

75. This form of "inalienable" is the one used by American Methodism's founders.

76. *Methodist Disciplines 1785–1789*, Library of Methodist Classics (Nashville: United Methodist Publishing House, 1992), *1785 Discipline*, 15.

77. Stephens, "A Witness of Words," 115; see the whole section, "Theological Commitments," 114-18.

78. *BODUMC*, 1988, 95.

79. *BODUMC*, 1988, 96.

80. "Though coercion, violence, and war are presently the ultimate sanctions in international relations, we reject them as incompatible with the gospel and spirit of Christ" (*BODUMC*, 1988, 108).

81. *BODUMC*, 2000, 119.

82. *BODUMC*, 1988, 109.

83. *BODUMC*, 2000, 121.

84. "Using Force to Overcome Evil" by James V. Heidinger appeared in the November/December 2001 issue of *Good News Magazine*; Roger Wolsey's letter appeared in the March/April 2002 issue; accessed at http://www.goodnewsmag.org/magazine/2MarApr/MA02LETTERS.htm (accessed March 20, 2007).

85. *BODUMC*, 2000, 119.

86. *BODUMC*, 1992, 89, 92, 93, 98.

87. *BODUMC*, 1996, 90, 97, 98.

88. *BODUMC*, 2000, 98, 103, 110, 111, 112, 115, 116.

89. *BODUMC*, 1992, 93.

90. *BODUMC*, 2004, 102.

91. *BODUMC*, 2000, 102.

92. *BODUMC*, 1972, 86; *BODUMC*, 2004, 102.

93. *BODUMC*, 1996, 102.

94. *BODUMC*, 1988, 95.

95. *BODUMC*, 1992, 92.

96. *BODUMC*, 1996, 87.

97. Under "Unauthorized Conduct" of ordained elders: "Ceremonies that celebrate homosexual unions shall not be conducted by our ministers and shall not be conducted in

our churches" (*BODUMC*, 2004, 241). Under "Chargeable Offenses": "conducting cere-monies which celebrate homosexual unions; or performing same-sex wedding ceremonies" (*BODUMC*, 2004, 719).

98. *BODUMC*, 2000, 101.

99. Judicial Council Decision 1032, which the Judicial Council declined to reconsider when it met in 2006 (*United Methodist Newscope*, May 12, 2006, 1).

100. *BODUMC*, 2004, 99.

101. In response to an *ABC News/Washington Post* poll conducted in June 2006, 65 per-cent of Americans said they favor the death penalty for persons convicted of murder. Accessed at: http://www.pollingreport.com/crime.htm.

102. *BODUMC*, 2004, 120-21.

103. *BODUMC*, 1992, 89-90.

104. *BODUMC*, 1996, 86.

105. *United Methodist Newscope*, June 30, 2006, 7-8.

106. E-mail communication from William Lentz to John G. McEllhenney, December 8, 2006.

107. "Immigrant Facing Deportation Seeks Sanctuary in Church," *United Methodist Newscope*, August 25, 2006, 1.

108. E-mail communications from Kent Kroehler to John G. McEllhenney, December 9, 2006, and January 6, 2007.

109. "New United Methodist Social Creed May Be Set to Music, Rap," *United Methodist Newscope*, May 5, 2006, 1-2.

110. *United Methodist Newscope*, February 2, 2007, 1.

111. E-mail communications from Neal Christie, associate general secretary of the General Board of Church and Society, to Charles Yrigoyen Jr. and John G. McEllhenney, June 14, 2006, January 5, 2007, and September 29, 2007.

112. See "Proposed Social Creed Seeks Global Acceptance," *United Methodist Newscope*, September 28, 2007, 1. This is the text of the draft Social Creed that the General Board of Church and Society will submit to the 2008 General Conference. Text sent to John McEllhenney by Neal Christie, an assistant general secretary of the board, September 29, 2007.

113. E-mail message from Neal Christie to John G. McEllhenney, January 8, 2007.

114. Kathy L. Gilbert, "A Social Creed you can sing?" United Methodist News Service, April 25, 2006.

115. Richey, Rowe, and Miller Schmidt, II:671.

116. Ibid., II:703-4.

117. "Scorecard: Who won and who lost on election day," *Christian Century*, November 28, 2006, 13.

118. Bob Edgar, *Middle Church: Reclaiming the Moral Values of the Faithful Majority from the Religious Right* (New York: Simon & Schuster, 2006), 2.

119. Ibid., 5, 1.

120. Ibid., 5-6.

INDEX